What You Need to Know When

Your Child Is Learning to Read

Sara Wilford

What You Need to Know When

Your Child Is Learning to Read

Sara Wilford

SCHOLASTIC INC.

New York   Toronto   London   Auckland   Sydney

Copyright © 1998 by Scholastic Inc.
All rights reserved. Published by Scholastic Inc.
Printed in the U.S.A.
ISBN 0-590-03291-7
10 9 8 7 6 5 4 3 2   01 00 99 98

ACKNOWLEDGMENTS

When you have many people to thank it's impossible to prioritize. That said, thanks first to my children and their extraordinary families, who urged me to write this book for parents, and to my husband, whose belief in me survived the mental absences that ensued. Thanks, next, to the colleagues whose encouragement and friendship sustained me in finding a voice: especially Charlotte Doyle for her unerring wisdom, Mary Hebron for her deep and sensitive reading of the manuscript, and the teachers at Sarah Lawrence Early Childhood Center—with special gratitude for May Kanfer's and Sonna Schupak's generosity in sharing examples of children's work. Thanks to fathers and mothers over the years who asked me crucial questions. And finally, thanks to all the "reading detectives": the children I encountered and loved in my years of teaching. They were—and continue to be—my inspiration.

For
Sara Elisabeth di Bonaventura

Contents

Foreword ii

Introduction iv

CHAPTER 1
Five Inside Stories 8

CHAPTER 2
The Building Blocks of Reading 24

CHAPTER 3
Children as Reading Detectives 40

CHAPTER 4
Becoming Your Child's Reading Partner 52

CHAPTER 5
Will My Child Have a Reading Problem? 67

CHAPTER 6
You and Your Child's School 76

Afterword
Reflecting on Your Child as a Learner 88

APPENDIX 1
Frequently Asked Questions 92

APPENDIX 2
Resources 95

FOREWORD

One of the enduring pleasures of my undergraduate years was the art history class I took as a sophomore. Squeezed in between organic chemistry and physics, both located across campus, art history was always worth the walk. What made the class so rewarding was the chance to spend an hour looking at beautiful things, and receiving expert help in looking at them. The help came in the form of a much beloved professor who practiced looking as a fine art, and who had a knack for allowing us to see, if only for 50 minutes at a time, through his eyes.

In *What You Need to Know When Your Child Is Learning to Read*, Sara Wilford, like my old art history professor, manages to combine a sophisticated understanding of her topic with a style of explanation that is, in the very best sense, simple. With the eye of a seasoned preschool and elementary educator and the ear of a storyteller, she illustrates her points with memorable examples and provides solid advice. She does not talk much about the extensive body of research that exists on the development of literacy, but her mastery of the subject shines through. Throughout, she insists on seeing each child as an individual and as a member of a family and a peer group.

As a pediatrician, I find this aspect of Sara Wilford's book especially gratifying. Temperament and a child's accumulated life experiences certainly color how he or she responds to the stress of a physical examination or immunization. These factors also shape how the child attacks the challenge of literacy. Just as different children learn to walk in very different ways —some cautiously, afraid to fall, others charging ahead without a care for bumps and bruises—so are there different ways to approach reading. How we understand those individual differences, and what we do as parents and educators to nurture individual children, is the core of Sara Wilford's book. It is a book about the development of literacy. But more fundamentally, it is about children and how they grow into themselves, with the help of adults who understand and support them.

Many have written about the stages through which children pass on the way to conventional literacy. None have described better the passion, seriousness, and delight of children as they make that journey of discovery, nor the variety of paths they take. It is a journey we have all made and for the most part forgotten. But those of us who have the privilege to care for children, personally or professionally, have an opportunity to make those discoveries again — through observing our students, patients, sons, and daughters. Sara Wilford has given us a guide-book for the voyage that is both practical and full of colorful detail. Like my old art history professor, she lets us see through her eyes, and, in doing so, enhances our own vision.

Robert Needlman, M.D.
Rainbow Babies and
Childrens Hospital
Cleveland, Ohio

INTRODUCTION

In my work with parents of young children over the past 25 years, two questions have surfaced again and again. The first is general, and understandable to anyone who is a parent: "Is my child okay?" The second is highly specific, sometimes implicit, but ever-present: "When will my child learn to read?"

This book is therefore written for you. Its aim is to assure you that your child will learn to read, although the paths to that end may look very different to each of you... as different as each child is from every other. Reading grows from the ongoing process of children learning more and more about language. Even as children are first beginning to speak, they are finding out about oral and written language from their observations of the world, from watching their parents and other adults, and from making personal connections to actions and things around them. For example, a fifteen-month-old looks at a photograph of a watch, listens to the ticking sound of her mother's wristwatch, then suddenly puts her ear to the picture of the timepiece on the page. Or a toddler sees the arches of a well-known restaurant chain and shouts, "McDonald's!" Events like these occur again and again on the continuous path that leads to children's independent reading, sometime around first grade.

To help you understand your child's learning-to-read adventure, Chapter 1 begins with five inside stories about five very different children who learned to make sense of print in their individual ways. Chapter 2 tells you about the foundational aspects in the process of learning to read—how does it all begin? Chapter 3 highlights your child's role as a "reading detective" in making meaning from print. Chapter 4 addresses ways in which you can become your child's reading partner. Chapter 5 takes a look at approaches to literacy learning and ways in which children learn to read in school. If you're concerned about your child's reading progress, the suggestions in Chapter 5 give you information about help that's available. Finally, Chapter 6 deals with the broader issues of working with your child's school.

The overall aim of this book is to provide insights that will empower you to support your child in becoming a successful reader in school and in everyday life and to help you acknowledge your child's individuality as a reader.

I share the following story with you as a stimulus for helping you recall your own process of becoming an independent and fluent reader. Reflecting back on your own style of learning is a helpful first step in recognizing how uniquely your child enters into literacy.

LISA'S STORY

One sunny Saturday morning in July, nine-year-old Lisa and her father set off on their weekend ritual of buying the family's breakfast doughnuts. Always on the move, Lisa sprints ahead with hair flying, cheeks flushed, and eyes a-twinkle. At the end of the block she executes a pirouette, looks mischievously over her shoulder in response to her dad's praise, and shouts, "Child genius!"

Lisa's father grins. He thinks to himself how good it is to hear his daughter's hard-won self-confidence. The road to this burst of pride has been uneven, much like the pavement on which she is now dancing.

As an infant, Lisa measured long. The oldest of three girls, she was inevitably the tallest child at home and nearly always the tallest in her class at school. A fussy baby and a headstrong toddler, her activity level was—and continues to be—high. Her parents' observations concurred with her pediatrician's assessment of her as a healthy child developing normally across the board. Her oral language was expressive, and she relished the books read aloud to her each night by her mother and father. Lisa attended a parent-cooperative preschool and entered kindergarten there just after her fifth birthday.

Lisa's kindergarten classroom reflected her teacher's understanding that five-year-old children need to be on the move and involved with activities. It was full of real-life materials, including a working stove in the large cooking area and a workbench with real tools. There were many books and a great variety of papers, markers, crayons, and paints. The room was alive with the voices of happy children who knew what they were doing. Ms. Broderick took pride in her children's independence and the growth she was able to document over the year. Lisa loved school.

However, in the spring, Lisa's parents were faced with the difficult decision of whether or not to enroll her in first grade for the coming year. They worried because although Lisa was tall, she was still on the young side and she couldn't seem to sit still for any length of time. When comparing notes with other parents, they discovered that many soon-to-be five-year-olds were already reading; Lisa, however, hadn't even started to read and had trouble writing her name. After several meetings with the principal and the first-grade teacher he recommended, Lisa's parents decided to enroll her in first grade, but not without apprehension.

During the primary grades at Hudson Elementary, Lisa continued to struggle with her handwriting and challenged teachers with her active temperament. But to her parents' delight, Lisa's teachers saw her urge for physical activity mirroring an intense curiosity, and they worked to help her channel her energies. As time went on, she proved to be a fine thinker with many interests and a special love for books.

Now, at the end of fourth grade, one of Lisa's greatest joys is reading. She uses books to find information about her many interests and to go on adventures to faraway places. Lisa has been a fluent reader since the end of first grade, but the story of how she made the transition from slow starter to fluent reader is uniquely her own.

Sara Wilford

1

Five Inside Stories

Recognizing Personal Approaches to Reading

W hen my eldest child began to read, sometime around the middle of first grade, I was both impressed and mystified by his extraordinary feat. While I expected that he would, of course, learn to read, I wondered what his teacher had done to help him make the connection between words and those puzzling black marks on the page. I never considered that my son might have unraveled the mystery for himself.

Years later, into the fourth year of my own first-grade teaching, I began to peel away some layers of the mystery of how children come to be readers. As I became more experienced, I realized there was a pattern to my students' progress. Consistently, about one third of my class entered as beginning readers, one third were all set to go, and one third showed little interest in learning to read. A small percentage of this latter third needed a careful assessment of why they were avoiding print and would most likely need some extra help. The large majority of each class, however, demonstrated that children came to school with personal reading timetables. If I respected these individual timetables, neither I nor they became anxious and reading evolved into a natural, shared happening within the classroom.

I structured my room and schedule to allow children opportunities to get involved in a variety of activities. This gave me more freedom to move around and get to know each child, time to listen to them talk and watch them at work. As I grew to understand the children better, it became feasible to use my knowledge to move them ahead, encouraging strengths and supporting areas that needed special attention. The classroom became a space where children were purposeful, an environment in which they could give each other the special kind of encourage-ment, challenge, and help that peers and a caring, insightful teacher can give.

The following portraits are drawn from my personal experiences as an early childhood center director and as a first- and second-grade teacher. I have chosen five very different children as a way of demonstrating the various strategies children use in learning to read. These are not case studies in the clinical sense, but true stories that shed light on the fallacy that all children learn to read in the same way. I've purposely underplayed the role of the teacher to give the reader a clearer picture of the *children's* role in problem solving.

Perhaps one of these stories will remind you of your own child's first attempts to make meaning from print. If so, the specific suggestions that follow each section may help you to build on your child's strengths while acknowledging his vulnerabilities.

KATHRYN
Enchanted by Picture Books and the Power of Stories

My most vivid mental image of Kathryn is that of a delicious three-year-old with a mop of curly hair, sitting cross-legged on the floor and intently reading *Blueberries for Sal* aloud. Oblivious of her audience, her total self was focused on the familiar pages of a book she loved, one that her parents had read to her time and time again. She turned the pages slowly from right to left, and her voice took on the quality of a reader as she recited the by-now-memorized text, emphasizing particular words and pausing in anticipation just before she flipped a page. Kathryn's words always fit the pictures on the pages she was looking at. Yet few of the sentences were accurate. It would be easy to see this performance as simply an acted-out drama of memorized lines. But it was so much more. The care with which Kathryn turned the pages, examined the pictures, and pointed to the print revealed her deep investment in the process she referred to as "reading."

> "And *so*, [page turn] the mommy bear
> went up the hill and Sal went
> behind her…
> Oh oh! Kerplunk! Sal dropped a
> berry in the pail!"

I was convinced that Kathryn would be an early reader. Both parents read to her every night, and during the day if time allowed. Books were an important part of this family's life. Kathryn loved books with predictable patterns, and after hearing *Freddie's Spaghetti* just once, she had been able to insert appropriate words without prompting.

> "Freddie ate…spaghetti
> And Freddie ate…spaghetti
> And Freddie ate…spaghetti
> Until it was…all gone!"

Kathryn also thrived on dramatic play. Alone, with friends, and with her little brother, she created dramas and acted them out with flair. In fact, Kathryn gave everything she related a storylike, almost conspiratorial, quality.

Kathryn's verbal abilities were strong. Her large vocabulary became richer as she matured, and she entered kindergarten as an older five-year-old. Her teacher soon recognized that Kathryn paid attention during group reading times and enjoyed most kindergarten activities, but she was both tentative and impatient when it came to reading in pre-primers that mostly used simple words with phonetic patterns (*Mat sat on his hat*). Did this mean that even though she loved books and stories, Kathryn was going to have difficulty learning how to read? Her parents, Maria and Walter, had some concerns but they did not pressure her.

Now that Kathryn is in first grade, Maria, Walter, and her teacher, Susan, have developed some hypotheses about her reading and writing behaviors. Because she has such an active imagination and deep love of story, Kathryn is impatient when she reads. She likes to substitute good words of her own to help make sense of the text. This is a strength—it shows that she will strive to make meaning from what she is reading—but it also causes her to skim over many words, ignoring details that will be important in the long run. Susan urges Kathryn to use her index finger to follow the text, and this simple strategy proves effective in slowing her down. Sometimes, she says, she thinks so hard that her mind "feels like a pretzel." Above all, Kathryn is working on her reading, achieving success with such tales as Dr. Seuss's *Green Eggs and Ham* and Bill Martin Jr.'s *Polar Bear, Polar Bear* because she loves these books and the stories that lie within them.

If Your Child Reminds You of Kathryn...

Remember that if your child is highly verbal, it doesn't necessarily mean that she'll be an early reader. It *does* mean, however, that she has a rich language base on which to build literacy skills. Here are some suggestions for making the most of her strengths:

- Create a book of her dictated stories for her to illustrate and share with others. If she feels you're writing down her words too slowly, show her how to dictate her stories into a tape recorder. Not only will she have an audiotape to play for friends, but you will have the stories to transcribe at your leisure and add to her special storybook.

- To help her build her reading vocabulary, vary your reading-time routines to include reading a chapter book aloud, having your child read to you from her current school or early-reading book if she's at that stage, and join in shared reading of a book you choose together ("You read one page [or paragraph]...I'll read the next."). Books with refrains or predictable sections can be particularly engaging. In all cases, it will be helpful to point out interesting or important words and to examine their details. Alternatively, you can play games in which you hunt for words with similar beginnings or endings or for words that rhyme.

- Provide your child with an easel and erasable markers or chalk, and keep them in your kitchen or family room. Encourage your child to experiment with writing. But remember, neatness is not your goal in this case; writing efforts are. Surprise your child with messages of your own! Use the easel for recipes and other real-life materials you can use for shared reading experiences.

CHRISTI
Building on Her Love of Writing

Christi began preschool in the threes class at our early childhood center. A serious child, she engaged in methodical painting, block building, and dramatic-play activities. While her oral language was developing normally, she was generally quiet and reserved.

As Christi moved through classes at our school, the teachers noticed progress: more social relationships, an obvious interest in activities, and a gradual willingness to engage in discussions with other children. As a four-year-old, she was certainly an observant child but still seemed somewhat taciturn and lacking in enthusiasm.

For kindergarten and first grade, Christi had the same teacher. This consistency appeared to foster an increased trust in herself as well as in her peers and her nurturing teacher. Adults who knew her still referred to her "somber" temperament. But she eagerly engaged in the more formal aspects of the kindergarten/first-grade program, playing math games with real pleasure and showing a keen interest in writing.

Letters—their shapes and sounds—were Christi's thing. She loved to write and used inventive spelling (spelling words the way they sound) to write her own words. She glowed as her stories got longer and longer and more and more complex.

SPOT   MIS   CHRISTINE

PEACH

WALTER

Her neat capital letter printing is typical of Christi's early first-grade work. Here is one of Christi's stories, written in the spring of her first-grade year:

THE MISTARY OF THE MISING BASBALL BAT

    WAS THAR WAS A GRAL AND HR NAME WAS JENAFR

SHE HAD A FAVRIT BASBALL BAT AND IT WAS

THE BEST BASBALL BAT SHE HAD

ONE DAY WEN SHE CAM HOME FROM SCHOOL IT WAS GON

HAV YOU SIN A BASBALL BAT

NO   NO   NO

          NO   NO

IM NEVR GOING TO GIV UP

NO ITS MI FAVRIT BASBALL BAT

I SE A BOY RUNING

PROBABL THATS HO STOL MY BASBALL BAT

HE FEL OVR AND A BAT FEL OT OF HIS BAG

THE PALES SO HEM AND HE WET TO JAL

The above story has a beginning, a middle, and an end. It has characters, action, and logic. Although there is no punctuation, there is evidence of Christi's ability to spell a number of words accurately. She also knows the verb ending *-ing*, as in *going* and *running*. Her sense of the sounds of speech is strong and she is not inhibited by long words, such as *mystery* (mistary), *Jennifer* (Jenafr), *favorite* (favrit), and *probably* (probabl).

One might think, given the evidence of her knowledge of letter sounds and words, that Christi would find learning to read an enjoyable experience. Alas! The very love of minute detail that went into forming letters and sounding out words proved to be Christi's greatest stumbling block. Instead of being able to use her considerable knowledge of whole words, word endings, and phonetic principles as reading strategies, she struggled through simple books word by word. She was so focused on individual letters and sounds that the meaning of the words, and the clues provided by the illustrations, were lost as she strove to decode each printed symbol. As she read, she pulled words apart into separate sounds—even words that she could write. It was painful listening to her. A simple phrase like

"'Mother Bear,' said Little Bear," became "Mm...o...th...er bb...ee... aa...er ss...ay...i...d ul...i...tt...ul bb...ee...aa...er."

Although her teacher tried to introduce Christi to other reading strategies, she continued to struggle.

By the end of the school year, Christi had made some progress, but it wasn't until the summer that she began to connect the words she was writing with the words she was reading. Now, Christi is as confident in her reading as she is in her writing. And she has made the transition from spelling words the way they sound to spelling words conventionally.

If Your Child Reminds You of Christi...

- Read with your child to build a general interest in reading. If she uses her finger to point to each letter, encourage her to sweep her finger underneath the word and blend the sounds to form a word. (Your goal is to help "c...a...t" become "cat.") If her frustration level builds while decoding a word or if she seems to be losing the meaning of the text, read the word for her.

- Provide her with her own special writing journal if she enjoys writing stories, and make time for her to read them back to you. Purposeful writing, such as making a grocery or other shopping list, can give you opportunities for shared reading in a different context. Use words from the list to make a "concentration" card game with pictures of produce items on half the cards and their corresponding names on the others.

- Continue to read favorite stories or new chapter books aloud. The flow of your voice and the naturalness of your expression will provide an important model for smooth reading.

CARLOS
Already a Reader

"Carlos can read," said his kindergarten teacher. "Carlos can read... already," added his parents. "What are you going to do to keep him motivated and challenged in first grade?"

This initial conference with Carlos's parents shed some light on when their little boy had started to read. He had always been a verbal child at home, but in nursery school, he was an observer more than a participant.

He chose to watch while the other children built with blocks, painted, or took care of domestic matters in the dress-up area. One day, as the teacher was reading him a story, he soberly pointed to a word in the book. "Curious," he said. "That says 'curious.'" He flipped a page. "See?" he said to the teacher, "and it says 'curious' here, too." Then, pointing to the word *George*, he slowly raised his finger and pointed again to a class list of children's names on the wall: "'George' here…and it says 'George' there, too!" The one sign of Carlos's early reading was that, at age three, he could clearly identify whole words.

It was still early in my teaching career, and I had never had a fluent reader in my class on day one of grade one. I scurried to the library during lunch period and shared my plight with Doris, our school librarian. "Help!" I cried. "Carlos's parents have told me he can read anything— newspapers, chapter books, nonfiction, *anything*. Give me some material for my classroom library so he won't be bored!"

Now, *bored* is a word I've never thought of as appropriate for children, who by their very nature are intrigued with the world. But in this case I could imagine Carlos skimming through my large collection of picture books and books for beginning readers and feeling frustration with their simplicity. Also, no matter how individualized my reading program might be, there were sure to be group times when the class and I would be engaged in reading-related activities inappropriate for Carlos's level of competency.

During the first week of school I asked Carlos to choose a book that he would like to read to me. He picked a short chapter book, quickly demonstrating both fluency and comprehension that were at least equivalent to a fourth-grade reading level. An undemanding child, he seemed completely comfortable as he curled up on a pillow in the library corner, eyes glued to one book after another.

On the other hand, writing was a different and difficult matter. Carlos's handwriting was shaky, and his interest in writing minimal. Then it hit me. Why, I asked myself, would he want to struggle with writing simple stories in a journal when reading much more complex texts was so much easier—and more rewarding?

With 24 other children demanding my attention, I tended to let Carlos read contentedly. This made me feel guilty, yet he seemed to be deeply interested in the wide variety of books by his favorite author I offered. Still, Carlos's parents' question echoed through me as I watched this proverbial bookworm in the cocoon of my library area: "What are you going to do for him in first grade?"

I got my answer one day when I noticed Carlos at a small table reading with one of his classmates. Since the other children all knew that Carlos was an accomplished reader, they often approached him for help with a difficult word or piece of text. On this occasion, Carlos and Lindsay were reading a story together—with Carlos doing most of the reading and Lindsay joining in when she could. "What a wonderful way to keep Carlos involved with the class while using his strengths as a reader," I thought to myself. From then on I encouraged Carlos to do more peer-tutoring (pairing a more able reader with a less able reader) while continuing to interest him in new books and authors. But it was my respect for Carlos's natural rhythm as a reader and his need for reflection that proved to be the best strategy for his future literacy. I know that he went on to become a superior student in many aspects of the curriculum and eventually achieved competency in writing, although reading would always be his first love.

If Your Child Reminds You of Carlos...

Keep calm. When children begin to read at an early age, parents are naturally very excited. Most probably, you have read to your child on a regular basis, and though it may not be obvious to you, he has been making connections about print. If it looks as though your child is already reading independently, you're not entirely off the hook! You need to think about ways of extending and balancing his accomplishments. For instance:

- Connect books to experiences and excursions that you share. For example, if you visited an aquarium and your child seems particularly interested in the shark tank, look for books in your library that give more information on sharks. Use these books as springboards for further discussion.

- Don't be surprised if your child loves to read but does not enjoy writing. Writing with a purpose, however, can be the key to building interest in this aspect of literacy. Encourage your child to share his interests with others by writing to them, whether in the form of simple story descriptions for friends, letters to loved ones who live far away, or correspondence via e-mail with a computer pen pal.

- Even if your child has started to read independently, continue to read to her from more complex chapter books that will engage her interest and increase her vocabulary. If she asks about the meaning of an unfamiliar word, not only explain it but point it out to her on the page as well. Most of all, keep in mind that reading aloud to a child is a special experience that can be enjoyed at any age or reading level.

Jamie
Determined to Put It All Together

On the first day of first grade, Jamie walked into the classroom, followed by his mother. He didn't stride in. He didn't sidle in. He simply walked in and took a good look around. One had the sense that he knew exactly where his mother was standing but that he felt free enough to stroll around the classroom and look at the different areas for exploration that had been organized by his teacher.

I was Jamie's teacher, and this was my first professional day in an elementary school. I had never taught first grade. I had never taught any grade. I had never taught anyone to read. And I was desperately trying to connect the names and faces of 25 children and 25 accompanying adults.

My reading program was planned around the idea that language experiences—reading to children, taking down and reading back their words and stories, and providing a library area with a large selection of books—would be the framework within which all the children could learn to read. But I was inexperienced in how to make this all work and had not taken into consideration the fact that children would invariably be at different stages in the learning-to-read process. Theoretically, I knew that all the children would have different styles and approaches, but I had not thought practically about how I might accommodate 25 individual modes of thinking.

Remembering Jamie that first day, I can now pick out clues to the way he was going to approach reading. He was independent. He showed curiosity. He demonstrated a propensity to observe carefully. And he liked to move freely within his environment. During the first weeks of school, I worked hard to use the children's own language, writing down their comments and observations about our class pet and other topics of interest to them on large chart paper. The children made picture books about their families, and I inscribed beneath the drawings whatever they chose to say about themselves and each of their relatives. I read them stories every day from our classroom collection of picture books.

Jamie would often go back to these experience charts and quietly examine them. He also spent time turning the pages of books in our library corner. The drawings in his personal family book were vivid, the captions short and simple; this book was the first that Jamie could read all by himself. During group activities with sounds and letters, Jamie eagerly joined in, and he loved rhyming and wordplay games.

During our one-on-one reading sessions, Jamie frequently chose a book in the "I Can Read" series called *Johnny Lion's Book*. He was able to read an occasional word, and I would read the rest to him. When I introduced the sequel, *Johnny Lion's Bad Day*, Jamie was enthralled. He began by getting to know the pictures really well and then asking me over and over again to read the text under the pictures that particularly intrigued him. He pestered me. He'd get a page just right, he thought, then come running over to make sure that *those* words on the page went with *that* picture.

Then one day, out of the corner of my eye, I watched Jamie do something that he had actually been doing for more than a week—only I hadn't taken in its significance. He was walking purposefully around the room holding *Johnny Lion Learns to Read* in his left hand, pointing at words in the book with his right index finger, and reading the words aloud at the top of his voice. None of the other children seemed to pay any attention to him. He was like a force, single-minded, persistent, intent on predicting and practicing the words he was coming to know. Jamie and his book were like a private world within the larger world of the classroom.

At the end of first grade, Jamie saw *The Wizard of Oz* on television and decided he wanted to read the book. He borrowed it from our school library. Although it was way beyond his reading level, he was not deterred. As with his beloved *Johnny Lion*, Jamie walked around our classroom loudly reading what he could from *The Wizard of Oz*, and when a word stumped him, he demanded help from me and the one or two others in the class who might be able to help.

If I could give a gift to every first-grade teacher, I would wish them a determined reader like Jamie. Through his persistence, practice, and willingness to take risks, he inspired me and made visible for every other child in the class the knowledge that learning to read can be both possible and pleasurable.

If Your Child Reminds You of Jamie...

- Using your child's own written work, such as a dictated story or message, highlight words that begin or end with similar letter sounds, belong to word families (*pet* and *met*), or have common endings like *-ed* and *-ing*.

- Make visits to your local library a regular part of your routine. All children gain from access to the library, and a child who is determined to find meaning in books will benefit greatly from frequent access to new volumes and interested persons, such as the librarian, who will take time to discuss the books. In between visits, make time to allow your child to practice reading to you. Be prepared for her to spend time pointing out words and commenting on their samenesses and differences.

- Use environmental print (words on signs, menus, package labels, and so on) to encourage word recognition in a variety of daily-life situations. The context will provide strong clues to unfamiliar words.

JOHN
A Late Bloomer

John had the face of an angel straight out of a painting by Raphael and the mischief-making capacity of Dennis the Menace. He had just turned six as first grade got under way, but exhibited the puppy dog quality of a younger child, tumbling around on the floor with any classmate who would join him.

As long as I provided choices, John was an agreeable, enthusiastic first grader. Group times and mandated tasks were quite another matter. John needed to move around in his own space and time, and asking him to conform with group routines for even short periods put severe demands on his threshold of self-control.

John showed an interest in stories read aloud but little motivation to independently examine the books in our classroom library. His drawings were primitive and his accompanying dictated stories sparse. By February, John was able to associate most consonants with their corresponding sounds and enjoyed writing his name and some short words to go with his pictures. He also showed interest in a series of pre-primers and primers I was using that year. I noticed that John confused some letters, particularly *b* and *d*, but I felt that his progress overall fell within the parameters of normal literacy development.

One day shortly after spring vacation, Ms. Gibbons, a special education teacher, asked if she could use my classroom as the environment in which to try something new. She wondered what it would be like to teach a whole class of children rather than the small groups she usually worked with in the Learning Center. After she spent some time getting to know the children, she conducted a group lesson reviewing letters and their sounds, and then she wrote some short-vowel words on the chalkboard. She asked for group responses, and got them. After this, she asked the children to write some words on their papers that she would say aloud.

I learned something important from watching the children's reactions—and from examining their papers. The children's success in writing the short words Ms. Gibbons had asked them to spell (*cat, mad, red, bed, dish, win, dot, rob, bun, nut,* and so on) varied widely. Some children, about a third, spelled all the words correctly. A larger group got nearly all the consonants right but missed some of the middle vowel sounds. A small group, four children out of the 24, appeared to have major difficulties with both consonant and vowel sounds and with letter formation. In examining John's paper I found that, despite his beautiful handwriting, he interchanged *b* and *d* indiscriminately, occasionally wrote *s* backward, and sometimes reversed the order of letters. For instance, John had written *bam* for *mad* by writing the word from right to left instead of from left to right.

Ms. Gibbons was concerned. She instructed me to have John work harder on his *b*'s and *d*'s and predicted that he would most certainly need extra help down the road. Did John and I work hard on those *b*'s and *d*'s for the remainder of first grade? You bet we did. I used every strategy I could think of to help him understand the differences.

We "talked" our way through the letters, John writing on paper, me tracing on his back with my finger: "*b*…down…up halfway…and around. Beautiful! *d*…start like a *c*… around…up… and down. Dynamite!" John made his own specially illustrated

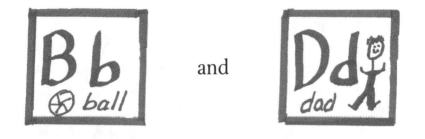

and

cards, which he taped to his desk. We made sandpaper letters for him to trace with his finger while saying "b" and "d." We created words using *b*'s and *d*'s from my collection of wooden letters. By the end of first grade his *s*'s were going the right way most of the time, but his *b*'s and *d*'s were as confused as ever.

As the teacher of the same group of children in second grade, I had John for another year. He returned from summer vacation a steadier, more focused child. Although still a hesitant reader, he did enjoy writing in his journal and reading from it to the class. John's family had just gotten a dog, and John was in love! His stories were simple and were all about his beloved pet. He quickly filled an entire journal with these stories and begged to begin another. However, John had a tendency to write hastily, without checking back over his work.

One day in early November, John's friend Tommy happened to look over John's shoulder while he was writing. "What's a bog?" Tommy asked.

"What do you mean, what's a bog?" answered John.

"There," Tommy pointed out. "See? It says 'bog.'"

"No, it doesn't, it says 'dog'!" John replied indignantly.

Back and forth they went. Finally, John's frustration with trying to get his classmate to understand his story led to a revelation. He now saw not only the similarity of letters like *b* and *d*, but also their differences. John realized that he needed to take extra time and care with his writing to be sure that others could read it.

For my part, I realized there were two crucial elements in writing his reversals away: time to mature and the impact of a peer's genuine desire to understand his story. Along with his writing, John's reading gradually became more fluent as he consistently showed success in blending the sounds of letters into words.

If Your Child Reminds You of John...

Take your child's general maturity level and need for physical activity into consideration as he enters a formal school setting. Some children have a young "feel" about them even at age five and six. To help him settle down to academic tasks in school:

- Provide him with after-school opportunities to let off steam or to play freely and quietly at home.

- Structure your reading time to allow for picture books and short books in which he shows an interest. As he approaches independent reading, ask his teacher to suggest books that will not frustrate him but will help build both his confidence and a growing sight vocabulary.

- If he likes to write, encourage him in whatever ways seem to intrigue him: drawings with captions, small books made from paper stapled together, or a journal.

- If your child reverses his letters, make a set of sandpaper letters for his own tactile reference. You can do this by drawing large block letters on squares of cardboard, painting them with glue, and sprinkling them with sand. Keep the letters in a labeled shoe box.

In each of the inside stories you have just read, a child took important personal steps toward literacy. Kathryn, who showed many behaviors manifested by early readers, began to read at age seven. Christi's interest in letters and sounds helped her move from fluent writing to fluent reading. Carlos's reading abilities emerged early, although for him writing was a struggle. Jamie came to school with a determination to learn to read and developed a repertoire of strategies (including lots of practice!) on his way to becoming a reader. And John is a good example of the proverbial late bloomer who, given the space and time to mature, makes slow but steady progress.

The preceding stories tell us that if we pay careful attention and if we are good observers, our children will enlighten us about the unique timing and strategies they have been developing since infancy to use and understand language. On the other hand, there are certain connections that every child needs to make to become an independent reader. The next chapter will introduce you to the foundational elements of reading that you can build on to help your child become a successful reader.

2

The Building Blocks of Reading

Connections Every Reader Makes

You're reading your child's favorite book aloud and suddenly he chimes in and starts reading along. Your child shows you a note she wrote and among the familiar scribbles you see a letter *t*. Entering a new classroom, your child points to her name on the cubby and says, "That's my name!" Your child is on the road to reading and making connections about the mysteries of written language.

Let's take a close look at how literary connections, like the blocks of a child's building, form a foundation for children as they become readers— and how you can help.

Acquiring and Using a Rich Vocabulary

Beginning in infancy, parents, grandparents, and caregivers interpret and respond to their babies' facial expressions, cries, and coos. This sensitive interaction sets up enormous anticipation of the child's first word and of the subsequent words that will soon begin to tumble out. Perhaps the first word is *mama* or *dada*. What an excited fuss we make over these early utterances!

> *"Listen! She said, 'Dada!'*
> *See, sweetie, there's Dada!*
> *Dada, look at Jenny!*
> *Jenny says, 'Dada!'"*

These enthusiastic responses acknowledge meaning built between the parent and the child, and before long Jenny not only looks at "Dada" when she says his name, but can point to herself and say "Enny." Children's vocabulary growth thrives on adults' natural excitement and desire to engage them in conversation. The more interest and time invested in talking to children, the richer their vocabularies will become.

Children also add to the growing number of words they understand and speak through playing with siblings and friends. The knowledge that words represent ideas and things is a powerful concept. When children focus their energies on "pretend play," they may fill a cup with invisible tea, ride an imaginary horse on a stick, become a cat or a dog prowling the floor with appropriate meows and woofs, or cook a clay chicken in the play oven. Through these actions we know that children understand the meaning of *teapot, horse, cat, dog,* and *chicken,* and have a wealth of ideas and actions to associate with them. They are using language to interact and communicate with others, as well as to shape and form their own ideas about their world.

Children learn an enormous number of words in the process of becoming fluent *speakers*. By the time your child is ready for kindergarten he can be expected to have a vocabulary of between 2,500 words and 17,000 words, with 7,500 being the average.

What You Can Do to Help

- Read and tell stories using a broad range of words. Children will acquire a rich vocabulary by listening to words used in context.
- Talk to your child! Long car rides, dinnertime, and trips to the grocery store are all opportunities for conversation.

Learning How Language Works

Your young child has not only learned and understood a large vocabulary of spoken words, he has also been absorbing the conventions of grammar and sentence structure.

It's easy to think of a little one's "Me do it myself!" as an adorable expression, but it is important to recognize it as a logically structured sentence. The child who can point to himself and say "me" demonstrates an understanding of the use of pronouns to begin a sentence. The child who says "I goed to the store" intuitively shows a firm grasp of a familiar past-tense form, and the three-year-old who responds forcefully to her mother's "Come here" with "I'm come-here-ing!" understands very well the use of participles.

WHAT YOU CAN DO TO HELP -------------------------------------

- Make sure to include your child, no matter how young, in all family outings and discussions that you judge appropriate. Food is always a great catalyst, so aim to make the most of talk around all the meals you share.

- Support your child's impulse for dramatic play. It involves so much more than a simple game of "just pretend." Dramatic play actually helps children come to understand themselves and how they fit in the world. Very young children engage in imaginative play beginning around age two, and good early childhood programs encourage this activity as a valuable opportunity for language development. Imaginative play can be fostered at home with simple props like pillows, pots and pans, and dress-ups.

- If your child enjoys storytelling or has a dramatic bent, consider using a video camera to capture and replay spontaneous dramas, staged alone or with friends. Viewing the videotape will give both you and your child pleasure, as well as providing a vivid record of developing vocabulary and language usage.

Understanding That Print Carries Meaning

Children with rich vocabularies are primed to bring meaning to print. Knowing that the car stops at the stop sign, and understanding what it means to stop, invests the sign with a message. They begin to grasp that the sign, with its large white STOP, stands for both a specific spoken word and a meaningful action.

Children who have been read to on a regular basis, who watch adults become absorbed in books, newspapers, and magazines, who take note of letters and postcards as they receive and send messages, and who grasp that the produce sign in the supermarket says "fruits and vegetables," are also children who know that print carries meaning.

WHAT YOU CAN DO TO HELP -------------------------------------

- Point out significant signs in your neighborhood. Your child can "read" the pictures and colors to find meaning.

- Be a role model by sharing your own meaningful reading and writing activities with your child.

Recognizing the Importance of Story

Story plays a critical role in how both children and adults learn to orga nize experience. The three-year-old who loudly announces, as her mother leaves for work, "Mommy's going to work. Mommy's going to work in her office. Then Mommy is coming home!" is telling an important story about her mommy's day, complete with the anticipation of their reunion. Pretend play, a game like hide-and-seek, using puppets, and telling each other what happened during the day are all opportunities for expressing stories. And every parent who tells or reads a story possesses the potential to inspire.

Stories in books contain the potential for making significant connections between children's life experiences, their developmental stages, and the pages of print. Every book holds some aspect of story within its covers. For very young children, the story draws in the listener with familiar events and enthralling pictures. As they listen, children add their own associations and feelings to a book.

Take Maurice Sendak's *Where the Wild Things Are*. This picture book is a wonderful example of blending fantasy and reality into a perfect story that children appreciate because it relates to their concerns about power and autonomy. It was an enormously controversial book at the time of its publication. Wouldn't tender young things be terrified by those illustrations of huge, scary monsters? the book's critics worried. But children knew better, and the book has become a timeless classic because of them. The book has also propelled many children into reading. The themes are powerful, the vocabulary accessible, the number of words per page perfect for remembering. And then there is the hero's name, "Max," a name that can be easily picked out on page after page.

WHAT YOU CAN DO TO HELP --------------------------------------

- It can never be said too often: Read aloud to your child on a regular basis. Bedtime is the preferred hour for most families, but don't let that keep you from other possibilities. For instance, while some parents need to unwind after a hard day's work, others like to reconnect with their children immediately, and sharing a book is both a cozy and a meaningful option.

- Let your child catch you in the act of reading. Almost all adults peruse the newspaper regularly, and this can be a valuable vehicle for sharing appropriate news items with children. Family reading times, when everyone chooses a book, a magazine, or (for the adults) work-related reading matter, can help children see the value of print in many forms.

- Encourage your child to tell you a story—it can be fictional or it can be a story of the day. And tell your child your personal stories. "When you were born, your head was so pointy..." Remember to include story elements like beginning, middle, and end.

Using Real-Life Experience

While some children gain an understanding of print through immersion in the world of stories, others may become deeply involved with print that connects them to their own everyday interests. The following story illustrates one way in which a child's love for something can help to build literacy connections.

Benjamin's family loved sports, particularly football, and engaged him in active play from the time he was a very little boy. In his large extended family, talk often centered on the particular game of the season, whether it was football, basketball, hockey, or baseball. The adults around Benjamin devoured sports magazines and the sports section of the newspaper.

Benjamin developed his own interests and enthusiasm, and sports soon became a main avenue for his process of learning to read. He built extensive collections of baseball and other sports cards, and invented multiple ways to use them in games of sorting and classifying, memorizing the players' names, teams, and statistics. Getting to the sports section of the newspaper first became a race between him and his parents, and a favorite copy of *Sports Illustrated* was dog-eared from use. A child who wanted to know all aspects of a task or a game before embarking on it publicly, Benjamin surprised his parents by quietly starting to read to himself somewhere between the ages of four and five. Benjamin is now a third-grader, and the details, heroes, and events of the sports world continue to engross him.

Benjamin's story reflects three aspects of the relationship between children's desire to access information and their ability to learn to read. First, his family both engaged him in sports activities and demonstrated their own interest through animated discussions and related reading matter. Second, because Benjamin wanted the information that would help him make sense of his passion, he worked hard to make the connection to printed words. What wonderful resources those baseball cards provided! The pictures helped him recognize the names of the players, his recognition of numbers helped him with the statistics, and his general knowledge of the game allowed him to hunt for other significant information about individuals and teams. Finally, Benjamin extended meanings by inventing games with his cards and practiced his emerging reading skills with the newspaper sports sections and his trusty *Sports Illustrated*.

WHAT YOU CAN DO TO HELP ---

- Include your child in planning for and researching family events. Invite him to cook a meal with you and show him how you use a recipe book (this may benefit his math skills as well). Allow him to help you use a map, train schedule, or tour book while planning a trip.

Reading Print in Everyday Life

What first informs us that a Big Mac is around the corner? Is it the arches or the word *McDonald's*? Our individual answers tell us something about how we read the world. Jane's father recently sat in my office reminiscing about his daughter's interest in cars.

Jane was crazy about cars. She noticed not only the colors but also the shapes (long back, long front, low to the ground). She noticed the taillights, the side mirrors, and the windshields. At four, Jane began to ask what the cars were called, and her mother and father would identify the makes. At five, Jane could identify most cars by sight, yelling out "There's another Honda!" Just after her sixth birthday, she insisted on hunting for any car label that wasn't immediately visible, matching the printed word with her knowledge of the make. Jane was a beginning reader, a reader of cars, with many long and complex words in her reading vocabulary, from which she drew numerous conclusions about the shapes and sounds of print.

A few short weeks after hearing the above account, I heard this story from three-year-old Barry's mother. Barry occasionally went into the city with his parents from their home in the suburbs. He loved riding the train. The station was a special place, and the evening ritual of picking up his dad at the train was the high point of his day.

One Saturday as his parents lingered over breakfast reading the newspaper, Barry shouted, "There's an *m*! "

"Where's an *m*?" Barry's mother replied.

"There!" exclaimed Barry, pointing to the back of his father's newspaper. Both parents scoured the back of the paper for an *m* and *n* big enough for Barry to recognize, but it was Barry himself who had to point it out for them on the folded-down side that had been exposed to him. "Look," he said, "an *m*! Like Metro North!" And sure enough, there on the reverse side of the paper were the words *News of the World*. Upside down, they had appeared to Barry as *M* and *N*.

Accounts like this remind us that each child is reading the world in his own way. Some look for detail, like Barry and his letters, and others at the big picture, like Jane and her cars. In a lovely little book called *When Will I Read?* by Miriam Cohen, you and your child can encounter a first-grader named Jim and his delightfully relaxed teacher, who has lots of things for children to do in her classroom. She writes down their stories and gives them plenty of time to play. One day Jim comes streaking across the room to report that the hamsters' sign is torn and now says, "DO LET THE HAMSTERS OUT."

"They could get killed!" cries Jim. As his teacher smilingly prints a new sign that reads "DON'T LET THE HAMSTERS OUT," she says, "I told you it would happen. You can read. That was reading. You really read that sign."

Jim was reading his classroom world.

WHAT YOU CAN DO TO HELP ---

- Become aware of the many ways in which your child can use the environment as a treasure trove of reading possibilities: signs on and inside stores, menus in restaurants, traffic signs (which may not have words printed on them but whose symbols hold meaning). Play games when you and your child drive or walk together—counting the number of exit signs on the highway, noticing names and numbers on mailboxes, and watching for special signs such as "SCHOOL," "CHILDREN AT PLAY," and "BEWARE OF DOG."

Moving From Scribbles to Letters and Words

Long before children can formally read and write, they engage in time-honored acts of imitation, which some adults call "pretending." At age three or four, a little girl scribbles across a piece of paper with her crayon. A little boy slowly turns the pages of a book, pointing first at the left-hand page, then at the right. From a superficial standpoint, these children are "just pretending" to write and read. But let's look beyond the surface.

From Left to Right

A little girl is making a series of marks that flow conventionally from left to right, and a little boy is turning pages and pointing to them in sequence. Both children have made basic connections between the way print moves across a page and the way a story progresses through a book. They understand that directionality, the movement of print from the left to the right side of a page, is a basic convention of literacy in our culture. And because writing and reading conventions are identical, both may be thought of as early reading behaviors.

What Are Those Black Squiggles?

Seeing the squiggles of printed text and then writing their own scribbles act as preambles to children's curiosity about *which* squiggle means *what*. In noting your child's emerging literacy, you'll find that a logical sequence of progress does not necessarily unfold.

The child who delights in line after line of scribbling often begins to insert occasional letters that stand for a word, though a particular letter may have nothing to do with the word it represents. A further step is to insert a word into a scribbled line. This may be an actual message or a playful use of words already in her writing vocabulary, combined with an imitation of the flow of adult handwriting. The illustration on the following page includes the members of Carolina's family—Pa, Baby, Mom—with Carolina's own name written down the right-hand side.

If your child loves to pore over his picture books, he may begin to focus on the pages' black squiggles and connect memorized text with the words, or conversely, the pictures may trigger specific words. Perhaps the sounds of letters intrigue him: A word may jump out because it begins with a familiar letter, and he may connect it to a word that he knows is on that particular page. Or maybe an oft-repeated word stands out because of its shape and length (such as *Max* in *Where the Wild Things Are*), bringing the first awareness of separate words.

Noticing the Details

If you or I decided to learn a foreign language with a different written notation, such as Russian, Greek, Hebrew, Japanese, or Arabic, we would face some of the problems young children tackle when they look at written English. First, we would need to find out about the conventions of that particular language: the directional flow of the writing (for example, Japanese is read from bottom to top and right to left), the meaning of the symbols, the connection of symbols to sounds, and how the words are arranged.

As children begin to look closely at the details of written English, they will inevitably pay attention to elements such as shape and size/ sameness and difference. Adults are continually amazed that young dinosaur buffs can recognize the words *Brontosaurus*, *Stegosaurus*, and *Tyrannosaurus* but continue to be stumped by those little words *and*, *the*, and *but*. Teachers of the primary grades (kindergarten, first, and second) have long understood the power of a child's interest in a subect in stimulating the desire to read. In the case of dinosaur names, not only are they meaningful and concrete, but their very length and shape make them stand out as unusual and memorable. The child who has an awareness of consonant sounds has some advantage in differentiating these words, but a visually oriented child has built-in strategies too. Let's look at the configurations:

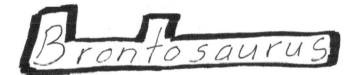

Although a child will almost never articulate how he is trying to decode a word, here are some strategies he might choose from in attempting to identify the dinosaur name *Tyrannosaurus*.

- It's a really long word.
- It begins with a big letter.
- It has *us* at the end like all dinosaur names do.
- It doesn't start with the curly shape (S) like *Stegosaurus*, or the big rounds (B) like my sister Barbara who has a name that begins like *Brontosaurus*.
- Maybe it's *Tyrannosaurus*?
- Mmmmm…It starts with a big, tall letter and one that has a kind of tail. That's the way I'll know which one it is.
- I'll check it out with an adult.

Of course, most children discover these exciting words by looking at pictures of dinosaurs in books or by exploring the dinosaur section in the museum, activities that supply them with dynamic clues to help them identify the words. If your child recognizes the word over time, in different books and in different places, then he is reading it—even if he cannot break it down into its component sounds. And one thing is sure. Any child who can recognize the big word *Tyrannosaurus* will have no trouble knowing that the little word following it is *rex*!

Natalie, a five-year-old kindergartner at the early childhood center I direct, was excited by the idea of chapter books, which were being read aloud to her kindergarten class. Natalie longed to read these chapter books to herself and begged her mother to buy and read the books to her at home.

Then Natalie found a set of primers in her house designed to teach English to Japanese adults living in America. Natalie studied these English primers, looking for similarities among the words, examining the pictures for information they might provide. One night during bedtime reading, to her mother's astonishment, Natalie began to read along spontaneously with the current chapter book. Eventually Natalie and her mother read pages to each other, until the little girl requested to read these much-loved chapter books "just by myself."

- To help your child see and sequence separate words, build a file card catalog of favorite (and useful) words that can be manipulated, illustrated, and put together to form simple sentences. Another tactic is to write down a story as your child tells it (write boldly with a marker on sturdy paper), then cut up the sentences and play around with sequencing them. When you think he's ready, cut up a sentence into separate words, and play again.

- Honor your child's experiments when writing, no matter what stage of writing development he's at. Remember that scribbling and the process of moving from scribbles to letters and words is one of the ways he is learning to read and write. Children often begin to insert words in their scribbles, as in the sample of Carolina's writing on page 32. *Pa*, *Baby*, and *Mom* are written from left to right, while the letters of her own name are strung from top to bottom on the right side of the page. Children enjoy playing with the shapes of letters, and sheets of unlined paper often give them the freedom they need for initial work on letter formation. Lined paper has its place later on, though many children can learn to write neatly on blank sheets.

- Books with accompanying audiotapes for young beginning readers can be helpful in several ways. If your child is still at the "reading the pictures" stage, he can turn the pages from right to left and follow the story along. Or you can sit with him and point to the words as the story unfolds. If he is beginning to read on his own, the audiotape can support his emerging fluency. The tempo and flow of the recorded voice will help him begin to make sense of punctuation.

Identifying Letters and Blending Sounds

In learning to read, children must be able to translate printed letters into sounds and to blend those sounds to form words. To do this, they need to be able to identify letters of the alphabet and the sounds they are associated with.

Educational television shows, such as the ever-popular *Sesame Street*, demonstrate how sounds and letters can be associated in meaningful ways, both auditorily and visually. Many children who have seen such shows enter school with good information about sound and symbol relationships. As a parent, you can encourage your child's development by playing rhyming games, singing songs, and listening to nursery rhymes together.

- Locate a set of sturdy plastic letters, uppercase and lowercase if possible. They can be used in any number of ways. If your child wants you to spell a word aloud, ask her to find and set out the letters she hears: This puts *her* in the driver's seat and gives you insight into what letters she can identify and how she orders them. Later, there will be opportunities for identification of capital and small letters and for play with making sentences.

- Build yourself a repertoire of phonic games. For instance, card games of concentration can be easily constructed by cutting out a set of tagboard cards: Paste pictures of familiar objects on half of the cards, and write their beginning (or ending) consonants on the rest. Make a collection of miniature plastic objects, such as fruits and vegetables or small toys, and play variations of "Find all the objects that begin with the s sound!"

- Remember that your child's own writing is a natural and meaningful way for her to practice sound-letter relationships. The attempts children make to spell difficult words, whether successful or not, show their growing abilities to represent what they hear and say in print.

Learning to Predict

Children who are read to either at home, at day care or school, at the library, or during educational television programs such as *Reading Rainbow* soon develop an intuition that written language is often different from spoken language. It has rhythm and pattern; it uses imagery; it may offer an unusual choice of words. Predictable books allow children to anticipate which words come next; this builds a tremendously helpful foundation for youngsters just starting to read.

Nursery rhymes for the littlest, chants such as "It's raining...it's pouring...the old man is snoring," and later, rhymes for jumping rope or playing "Miss Mary Mack" set the stage for the role of prediction in learning to read. Stories and storybooks with recurrent rhyming sections give children a sense of what comes next. In her book *Millions of Cats*, Wanda Ga'g begins with a familiar story opener, one to be found in many classic fairy tales.

> *Once upon a time there*
> *was a very old man and*
> *a very old woman.*

Soon we are introduced to an opportunity to predict—the very old man's discovery of a hill "quite covered with cats":

Cats here, cats there,
Cats and kittens everywhere,
Hundreds of cats,
Thousands of cats,
Millions and billions and trillions of cats.

This refrain is repeated with slight variations throughout the book. I dare you to find me a child who, after several readings, will not be able to fill in words at predictable points of this seemingly unpredictable story!

WHAT YOU CAN DO TO HELP --

- Collect, read, and reread books with rhyming lines or phrases into which your child can insert predictable words. This shared activity is not only fun, it often provides a window to poetry.

Recognizing the Language of Literature

One of the most frequently read books enjoyed by very young children and their parents is Margaret Wise Brown's *The Runaway Bunny*. Popular for its reassuring message that Mommy will always be able to find you, even if you run away, it has been a classic since its publication in 1942. A portion of the text highlights how book language differs from everyday speech.

"If you become a rock on a mountain high above me,"
said his mother, "I will be a mountain climber,
and I will climb to where you are."

"If you become a mountain climber,"
said the little bunny,
"I will become a crocus in a hidden garden."

"If you become a crocus in a hidden garden,"
said his mother, "I will be a gardener. And I will find you."

There is a rhythm to the words and a poetic imagery in the writing that clearly set the text apart from the way people usually talk. Although the child listener certainly knows how to play hide-and-seek, it is doubtful that he would say, "I will become a crocus in a hidden garden." Yet he loves the book. Its soothing rhythm and its metaphoric word pictures and illustrations have conveyed comfort, pleasure, and the germs of literary appreciation to many generations of young children.

Children can understand and appreciate good books that are far above their independent reading level and may be above their emotional maturity. While debating whether or not to read aloud a great children's book like E. B. White's *Charlotte's Web*, you may ask yourself if you feel your child is ready to deal with the sadness of Charlotte's death. But you will weigh the answer to that question alongside the power of the writing. In the following deceptively simple passage, White expresses the essence of the chapter's title:

LONELINESS

> The next day was rainy and dark. Rain fell on the roof of the barn and dripped steadily from the eaves. Rain fell in the barnyard and ran in crooked courses down into the lane where thistles and pigweed grew. Rain spattered against Zuckerman's kitchen windows and came gushing out of the downspouts. Rain fell on the backs of sheep as they grazed in the meadow. When the sheep tired of standing in the rain, they walked slowly up the lane and into the field. Rain upset Wilbur's plans.

Yes, book language *is* different from spoken language. It is important for children to know this as they approach the challenges of learning to read. Beyond the words lies the art of good writing—the fun and pure pleasure, the deep feelings and meaningful messages. Literature catches the child in its web, as Charlotte the spider catches her prey, and spins not only a story but the desire to become a reader.

WHAT YOU CAN DO TO HELP --

• Read books aloud to your child that bring *you* real pleasure! There are few things as compelling as hearing a book read by someone who enjoys both the language and the story. Your delight in reading, be it poetry or prose, picture or chapter book, sharpens your child's intuitive sense that written language often has a different cadence and rhythm than speech does.

• Encourage your child to tell you just *why* he likes a particular book or story. This will provide you with opportunities to talk about the language, the characters and the plot, and to get him thinking about the elements of good literature.

The literacy connections we have just explored are all necessary understandings children must arrive at to become fluent, independent readers. Children will have an easier time making certain connections than they will others. As you observe your child crossing the bridge to reading, you can become a partner in the process by using some of the suggestions at the end of each section and trying out some of your own ideas. All the while, you can be sure your child is playing his own part, like the "reading detectives" you'll meet in the next chapter.

3

Children as Reading Detectives

Using Clues to Uncover Meaning

Learning to read involves more than just deciphering words on a page—it entails children's search for meaning in print. As we saw in the last chapter, learning to read involves the intricate and individual blending of a set of literacy connections. These literacy connections don't just "happen"; they come about because your child is a problem solver and, in the particular case of written language, a "reading detective."

The common thread that connects all children's approaches to learning is their natural desire to investigate and make sense of the world around them. And print in all its forms and sizes—in books, on products and signs, or flashed across a TV screen—is very much a part of their world.

Children are thinking and detecting all the time. Learning about how your child acts as a reading detective will give you insight into how she thinks and learns. To find out more about the vast array of strategies children use, let's look closely at some real-life examples of children's problem solving as they learn to read.

A READING DETECTIVE
FINDS MEANING IN PICTURE BOOKS

I often hear parents say that their children think they are reading picture books, "but really, they're just memorizing." The following sequence looks closely at what "just memorizing" may mean and what it can lead to, using the example of a classic picture book, Margaret Wise Brown's *Goodnight Moon*.

Reading the Pictures

A child picks up the book, turns it right side up, and opens to the first pages of illustration. "In the great green room," she begins in a dramatic voice. Then, pointing to the pictures, she exclaims, "There was a telephone!…and a red balloon!…and a picture of [flip] the cow jumping over the moon!"

She continues reading with good, if not 100 percent, accuracy through to the final page and announces, "I read it all by myself!" We, astute observers that we are, understand that this is true. She has read the pictures.

Noting the Difference Between Pictures and Words

A reading detective notes that there are not only pictures in *Goodnight Moon*. There are pages with black squiggles on them.

A preschool child may already know that these black squiggles are words. The words may have been pointed out to her as a parent ran an index finger under the words while reading aloud. Now the child may begin to connect these squiggles with the meaning of the story. And she may begin to see similarities and differences between them.

Identifying an Important Word

Once a child understands these concepts of print, she will begin to identify individual words in text. "I know that the word *goodnight* comes here… [flip] and here…[flip] and here! It's a long word when you say it," she thinks. "Maybe it looks long, too. Well, this word is long…and it starts with the letter *g* like *go*. Go…goodnight. That must say 'goodnight'!"

Developing a Sight Word Vocabulary

Before long, the reading detective has added all the words on the pages, starting with the word *goodnight,* to her reading vocabulary.

"This has to say 'room' because it comes with the picture for the Goodnight room. And this says 'moon.' And this says 'cow'…and 'light'… and 'bears'!"

This child is now the undisputed master of a literary work. To achieve this feat, she has used her knowledge of language, her memory, her visual powers of observation, and above all, her resourcefulness in problem solving.

Though not a universal process, the preceding is one possible approach to noticing the difference between pictures and words while learning to read a favorite story.

WHAT YOU CAN DO TO HELP --

• Read picture books with your child often and early.

• Point out the conventions of print. "Look at all the words on that page" or "Hmmm, look at the bubble coming out of his mouth. He must be saying something."

• Encourage your child to "read" books aloud with you.

A READING DETECTIVE FINDS MEANING BY EXPLORING PERSONAL INTERESTS

Many children are spurred to understand print through a persistent interest in uncovering information. In *Speaking of Reading*, a collection of personal responses to the question "What is your reading history?," two reflections stand out that give vivid testimony to the incentives provided by a strong interest.

Rosa Coupe, the eldest of 17 children, grew up in Guadalajara, Mexico. Although she left school at nine to help care for her siblings, she has always been a good reader. Rosa muses:

> Maybe I could read because I always enjoyed cooking and reading cookbooks. My grandmother was a wonderful cook. And I always looked for recipes in magazines. I guess I put one and two words together and figured out the recipes or I asked people, "What does this word mean?"

Today, Rosa lives in the United States. She says, "I read newspapers, true stories in magazines, books. I have a few prayers I (brought) from Mexico. And if I'm going to be doing some cooking, I (use) three or four of my cookbooks (to) look for recipes."

In another account, Bill Costello (like Benjamin in Chapter 2 of this book, whose love of sports introduced him to reading) credits a family member as well as his own passion for baseball with his reading development. He classifies himself as a "baseball savant," and claims that he has read more books about baseball than anyone on earth!

> When I was seven I got interested in baseball the way a lot of people get interested in it, from my dad. He wasn't much of a reader since he only had an eighth-grade education, but he did read the sports pages in the newspaper. I remember him sitting with his coffee and reading the baseball scores to me. Sometimes we would each take a different paper and read each other baseball stories back and forth.
>
> I have to credit the game of baseball for my ability to read because the first book I ever read was a rule book—I wanted to know the rules, so I got a rule book and read it, and from then on I read about baseball on my own. I started subscribing to the *Sporting News* when I was nine, so I read that, and eventually, whole books about baseball. My reading had nothing to do with school; baseball was my total focus, my only interest.

IF YOUR CHILD HAS A SPECIAL INTEREST

- Visit the library together to read about your child's favorite topic. Both fiction and nonfiction selections may interest your child.
- Create cards with the specialized vocabulary of your child's area of interest. A set of baseball or dinosaur cards can be used to play matching or memory games.
- Encourage your child to create a simple book about her subject—to draw a volcano and write or tell about it.

A READING DETECTIVE
FINDS MEANING THROUGH WRITING

Many young children make connections to reading through their experiments with writing, although when and how they become interested in putting a drawing or writing implement to paper will vary. I have seen infants with pencils grasped in their fists making marks and watched toddlers experimenting with pastels. Each child evolves into a writer differently. One five-year-old may ask for "real homework" while another is concerned about her letter formation.

There are physical differences involved in writing, as well as temperamental differences. For instance:

- Right- or left-hand dominance may take a number of years to surface, slowing down the process. (Be aware that some children are legitimately ambidextrous).
- Hand-muscle strength develops slowly for some children, more rapidly for others.

Writing is much more than letter formation. Current research shows that young children deliberately explore written language through experimentation, turning letters into drawings and shaping letters in different ways. Some children love to practice making letters and will do so for long, uninterrupted periods of time. Others have uncertain pencil grips and struggle to conquer letters like *b*, *d*, *p*, *q*, and *s*, but they may like to draw, and drawing often leads to writing. They can be encouraged at each stage of their writing development if adults remember that every effort is an active step toward more and more discovery about creating print.

The following glimpses of young children in the act of writing will give you a feel for how these connections may proceed and build on each other.

A Single Stroke Stands for a Letter

Three-year-old Abby loves to sit with a pencil and paper and write the names of anyone who will indulge her. The process goes like this:

Abby: Nana…Want to write Nana!

Nana: Okay, Abby…N.

Abby (making a single pencil stroke on paper): N…

Nana: Then…A.

Abby (making a second stroke): A…

Nana: Another N.

Abby (making a third stroke): N…

Nana: And another A. That's it.

Abby (making a fourth stroke):
    A…I writed it! Nana!

Abby's parents are worried because she doesn't know the names and shapes of her letters. But she does know that each letter is a separate, single mark, and she is able to demonstrate that knowledge.

Scribbles Carry Meaning

A group of four-year-olds are making pizza with their teacher and taking orders for the toppings. Several carry small notepads and pencils as they move around the room canvassing to determine their classmates' preferences.

Tommy: Angie, What d'ya like on your pizza?

Angie: Cheese! And sausages.

Tommy (scribbling rapidly from left to right on pad):
　　Okay, cheese and sausages.

As Tommy goes from child to child, he records their orders seriously and industriously. Is he "just pretending" to write? In one sense, yes. But Tommy is also showing that he understands that print flows from left to right and that it means something. He will be able to look in his notebook and recall that the scribbled lines stand for all the different pizza toppings requested by his friends.

Marks and Scribbles Become Letters and Words

Often, the first word a child undertakes to write is his name. If there is one supremely meaningful word, your name is it! It needs no surrounding text to make a statement: You are the whole story! Other words soon follow, such as *Mom*, *Dad*, and the names of other family members. This personal writing vocabulary is often connected to drawings or paintings and forms a basis for further writing development.

Many children enjoy imitating the writing opportunities that occur in daily life, such as writing a letter, making lists, or taking notes during a phone conversation. Children who have some understanding of print concepts, and can hold a crayon, marker, or pencil with reasonable comfort, nearly always become engaged in meaningful writing activities they have seen modeled at home. In her delightful book, *Gnys at Wrk*, Glenda Bissex traces the development of her son's writing from scribbles to signs, lists, and readable notes. ("GNYS AT WRK" was a sign her son attached to his door in order to ensure "the genius'" privacy.)

If your child shows an interest in experimenting with writing, it means she's involved in high-level thinking that shows she understands there is a way to communicate with others beyond spoken words. She will write her first words using letters that represent the most prominent sounds she hears—in most cases, consonants. As vowels are included, which ones she uses will also be a reflection of what she hears, along with her growing understanding of vowels with their short and long sounds and variations. In many cases, children who are writing words, however partial, will be able to read them back, and this kind of transitional spelling can be a powerful key to reading.

Children's efforts at writing and their dictated comments can be effectively combined. The following examples, taken from an early childhood classroom, show how children's writing may develop. Although the children demonstrate individual styles and approaches, each example illustrates a desire to convey meaning—and giving and getting meaning is the cornerstone of learning to read.

JAKE: Writing Begins With His Name

Although the roar of an airplane in flight is Jake's favorite sound, his name is the central feature of a response to his teacher's question, "What sounds do you like?" He has also drawn a picture of an airplane and written the other important word in neat capital letters, using the sounds he hears. Notice that he separates the syllables, writing *ar* for "air" and *plan* for "plane." He assumes that *a* has a long *a* sound, and does not yet know that *ai* sounds like a long *a* or that a silent *e* is needed to make the long *a* sound in *plane*. Jake's teacher has helped him formulate a story by prompting him with a question and recording his response.

CAROL: Writing Is Motivated by Her Interests

Carol's class is investigating dinosaurs, and each child has chosen a favorite. Carol has drawn a Tyrannosaurus rex and carefully labeled her picture with the dinosaur's name. Far from being deterred by the word's length, Carol has correctly identified all the consonants. Working to hear the vowels, she makes logical selections, including *i* for *y* in the first word and an *e* for *rex*. She wants others to know the name of her preferred prehistoric reptile.

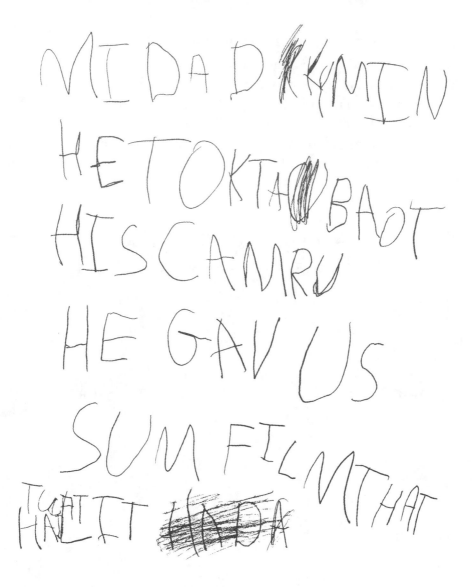

CARVER: Writing to Tell a Story

Carver writes an account of his dad's visit to the classroom. Using bold capital letters and transitional spelling, he writes, "My dad came in. He talked about his camera. He gave us some film that had light to it." When unsure of a letter or displeased with letter formation or word placement, he freely crosses out. Using consonants with accuracy and experimenting with vowels, Carver has written three sentences to tell others about an event that is very important to him.

NICOLE: Experimenting With the Conventions of Print

Nicole's class has a pet rabbit, and the children are keeping notes on her behavior. First, Nicole draws a picture of the pet in her cage with a bowl and water bottle. Then she writes about three of the rabbit's favorite foods and also notes the animal's water consumption.

Nicole lets us know that she has written this observation all by herself. Her writing shows a firm grasp of consonant sounds and identification of several vowel sounds, and she spells a number of words accurately. She is thinking about the roles played by punctuation marks, and she places a period between each word to denote its separate status.

ANNA: Gaining Mastery Allows a Complex Story to Emerge

Anna takes pride in her writing fluency and is moving toward a sure use of both capital and lowercase letters. Her story about her class's Thanksgiving feast is rich in detail and personal comment. She chooses interesting words and spells with a high degree of accuracy. Anna's story is punctuated with correctly placed periods and exclamation points.

Our thanksgiving
feast!

We invited MRS. KANfer's and they
class for sweet potatoes.
brought cranberry sauce and
corn-bread We all had fun and
the food was good to some
but not all I thougt that
that the sweet potatoes were
not suitable for my taste buds
espacally with marshmellows.
I Don't Think that the cranberrie
Sauce did either.
the end!

by anna

These writing samples demonstrate children at different stages of figuring out the conventions of writing. It is interesting to note that the children's ages do not correspond sequentially to the increasing complexity of the writing samples, although they were all either five or six years of age. The children were each proud of their work and could, without exception, read it back to others.

WHAT YOU CAN DO TO ENCOURAGE WRITING -----------------------

- Allow even very young children to experiment with writing. A toddler's drawing can be a fulfilling first voyage into the world of print.
- Create opportunities for your child to practice writing. Thank-you notes and lists provide real-life reasons to write.
- Listen while your child reads to you from his transitional spelling. Most children are able and eager to read what they have written.
- Don't forget: Scribbles count!

Reading detectives are at work all the time. This does not imply that adults have a minimal role in the learning-to-read process. Every picture book you introduce, every piece of paper and writing tool you provide, the interests you respond to, and the stories you read or tell are all crucial ingredients in your child detective's reading adventure.

4

Becoming Your Child's Reading Partner

Knowing What You Can Do to Help

Without question, literacy is critical for success in today's society. Knowing what you can do to support your child's emerging literacy will help you to become her partner in the process of learning to read.

The first step is to take a moment to observe every aspect of your child. What does she like to do best? Does she have an active or introspective temperament? In what areas does she demonstrate competence? Thinking about your child as a whole person will help you understand the way she approaches reading. Don't be intimidated by advice about the "right" way to learn to read or by the child next door who learned to read a year ago. Do remember that your child has already accomplished some incredible feats: speaking in complete sentences; running, skipping, jumping, throwing, riding a trike or bicycle; becoming curious and excited about the world. Also keep in mind that every child achieves these milestones at an individual pace. Some children learn to walk early and speak later, or vice versa! But there will be a period of "evening out"—and those who begin later do catch up.

OBSERVING YOUR CHILD'S LITERACY DEVELOPMENT

Each reading or writing effort, each comment related to print that your child makes, can be a clue to what she already knows or the way she's beginning to read. Your first task will be simply to observe and possibly also to record what your child already knows about reading. (One good way to document your observations is to keep a "literacy journal.")

Observing everything, from recognition of occasional words (such as chance comments about signs on the road) to stabs at writing (like Abby's in an earlier chapter), will help you know more. Then you can use your growing store of knowledge to support your child's own strategies. For instance:

- If she likes to draw, make sure there's a good supply of paper and crayons or markers; for the very young, drawings are stories.

- If she wants to read a scribbled story back to you, listen respectfully; she knows that writing can be read back!

- If she announces "I know! That sign says STOP!," encourage her by pointing out similar signs with "I see another sign" (rather than putting her on the spot with "What does that say?").

- If she has a passionate interest (horses? ballet?), provide books that intrigue and supply good information.

The more you know about how much your child already understands and is curious about, the more effective a partner you can be.

READING TO YOUR CHILD

There is no substitute for a child's first experiences with that concrete object called a book—smelling the aroma of the pages, rubbing fingers along the binding, feeling the smoothness of glossy paper. Nor is there a substitute for the positive feelings transmitted to a child by a reader who cares and who invests books with a personal value.

When you read to your child, you give the following very real and concrete gifts that encourage reading:

- Warm feelings aroused by the closeness between you, the reader, and your child, the listener.

- The chance to explore connections between your child's interpretation of the story and the actual story in the book.

- The desire to find out "what happens next" in the pages of a book.

- The realization that the black marks on each page carry meaning, allowing the story to progress and the child to revisit certain words, pages, and story events.

What Kinds of Books Should I Read?

It's never too early to read aloud to your baby, toddler, or preschooler. Board books are fabulous inventions for the littlest, because they allow for endless playing, holding, chewing, and turning of pages without damage to either book or child. Preschoolers, as well as older children, love picture books, which lend themselves splendidly to goodnight rituals. If at all possible, allow plenty of time before going to sleep to read and pore over beautiful and appropriate picture books. Many picture books are printed in paperback, but it's a good idea to share some hardcover books with your child as well, to allow her to experience books of different textures and sizes. (Holding *Peter Rabbit* in its original version, which was specifically designed by Beatrix Potter for tiny hands, is a very different experience from holding a larger version.) Your local librarian and your local bookstore will be glad to help you find and browse through books suitable for your child's age.

The school-age child still loves picture books, but you'll want him to begin actually reading text with you. Cozily settled with child in lap, you might draw your finger across the page under the words you are reading. Predictable books with rhyming text are especially helpful if you and your child enjoy this experience, because they make it easy for the child to guess what will happen. For example, if you are reading Bill Martin Jr. and John Archambault's *Here Are My Hands*, you may expect the following:

Parent: "Here are my hands
                for catching and throwing.
                Here are my feet
                for stopping and…

Child: …Going!

Your school-age child is also able to understand and appreciate chapter books and good books that are above her independent reading level.

When you choose a book to read aloud, think about the content, the language, and the experience the two of you will share. Does the book seem appropriate? Do you like it yourself? Do you consider it to be good literature or a factual book with well-written content? If the answers to these questions are all yes, don't hesitate to read the book aloud. Rich vocabulary, plot, and concepts can be assets rather than impediments to comprehension. Although your child may not understand every individual word, she will stretch to get the overall meaning of the story.

By my third birthday I would read the newspaper aloud to my mother in the mornings and had started reading chapter books for older children. I think that had I not been taught to read at such a young age, I would have taught myself around the same time just because I loved books so much and wanted to be able to get the stories out of them myself. The only thing I think was negative in my learning to read so early is that other people stopped reading to me once I could do it myself. I think that even though I didn't need to be read to in order to understand a story, it still would have been valuable for the time spent with adults who were important to me. —Erin DeMund, college student

READING WITH YOUR CHILD

It creeps up on you, nagging, creating doubt. Anxiety! It's one of the hidden stumbling blocks to productive reading with your child. I have experienced it both as a parent and as a beginning teacher, waiting breathlessly while the child beside me struggled to identify a word in a text that by that time had grown meaningless to both of us! These moments dampened the child's interest, blocked the child's ability to use strategies already in place, and made me feel helpless and frustrated. I later realized that the frustration I felt stemmed from my uncertainty about my own repertoire of strategies and a fear that any intervention on my part might only make things worse.

You will undoubtedly develop your own special mechanisms for reading with your child, depending on the speed with which she reads, your own tolerance, and your experience. Nonetheless, it helps to have a few tried-and-true tools in your back pocket. Here are some that work for me.

Helping Out With Those Tricky Words

If your child is reading aloud to you and gets stuck on a word, it's a good idea to wait patiently for a short while to give your reading detective time to make a good guess through context, analyzing the shape and length of the word, putting together the sounds of the letters, or using a combination of all three. If you sense that the process isn't working, then there is absolutely nothing wrong with supplying the word before frustration sets in. This will prevent the meaning of the sentence from getting lost, and encourage the reader to continue.

Underlining With Your Finger

Children who are just beginning to feel the thrill of recognizing words, or who are in the first stages of connecting memorized text to the printed page, tend to show tremendous concentration. This may be a good time to keep your finger under the word in question; it shows that you value what is happening and reinforces your child's ability to make connections between specific words and other parts of the text.

Don't be surprised, however, if your child races ahead of your jumping finger or slurs several words together while you hopelessly try to point to one at a time. Though not always satisfying for you, your involvement shows support and approval. As fluency increases, it's a good idea to slide your finger along smoothly across the page under the words as they're read. This supplies continuity, reinforces left to right orientation, and encourages comprehension of meaning.

Finding Phonics Opportunities

As your child begins to use his phonics skills, he will be sure to come across a word that seems impossible to decode. Use your judgment about how long to wait before supplying the unfamiliar word. Remember, your ultimate goal is to keep the meaning moving.

The child who wants to read for meaning and is using phonics strategies will have already narrowed the possibilities of an unfamiliar word down to a few words that begin with and/or end with the same letter as the unfamiliar word. This can be a ripe moment to introduce a new phonic pattern. For instance, take the sentence "Hannah went to see what mischief she could make." The word *mischief* could well hold up a beginning reader. "Mis...c...c...c..." she says. This gives you the opportunity to appreciate her decoding of the first part of the word and to take a look at the second part separately. "*Ch* makes a *ch* sound and *ie* makes an *i* sound in this word. So the second part of the word says 'chiff.' Let's put it together: 'mis...chiff.' What is 'mischief'? Let's go back to the beginning of the sentence and see how it fits in." In this case, two reading strategies—decoding and context—were used together to make meaning from the text.

UNCOVERING WRITING

Thinking about writing as the flip side of reading can help you to encourage and understand pre-writing and early writing efforts.

Supplies

Most children paint, scribble, and draw before they attempt to write words. All of these activities are significant steps that precede writing itself. This is why it's a good idea to keep a generous supply of paper and writing or drawing tools nearby.

Acting as Your Child's Scribe

Children who are tentative about experimenting with writing love to have their stories and ideas written down by interested adults. For these youngsters, pictures become frequent jumping-off points for a dictated caption or commentary. Letters and cards to loved ones—grandparents, aunts, uncles, friends—provide good opportunities for you to ask your child what she'd like to say and to transcribe the message word for word. This writing then becomes material to be read and reread.

And letters and cards you receive contain new and meaningful messages that you can read together.

When Writing Opens the Door to Reading

For some years now I have been using a first grader's handwritten, illustrated story to help primary-grade teachers figure out what children know about reading and writing. The particular child-author you are about to meet was not an early reader. He was an active child, interested in his environment, and trusting of the adults at his school. He did not worry about "correct" spelling or perfect handwriting.

Andrew liked to draw, and he liked to write. Here is the question I ask my teacher colleagues and the question I pose to you: Exactly what did Andrew have to know to write his story and to read it back to others? In other words, what did Andrew know about the adult term "literacy" that enabled him to express himself and create a brand-new scenario for one of his favorite *Sesame Street* characters, Big Bird?

Now, here comes the hard part: Do not look at the tiny translations at the bottom of each page (unless, of course, you are totally stumped). Instead, work at reading Andrew's book. And then ask yourself what Andrew had to know in order to write it.

Big Bird goes to have fun biking

What should I do said big bird while stepping out of his nest

I NO HE SAD
IAL GO BIKEG

I know he said
I'll go biking

HE GAT DRESt
WEL AMAG-NG
HEM BIKEING

He got dressed while imagining him biking

He went biking
There were lots of people
There was a little boy
standing nearby

HE SA tHE
ISK REMtRAK
HE WAKt OVE tOO Et

He saw the
ice cream truck
He walked over to it

HE WAKtAWA
WEtH HES
ISKRE KON

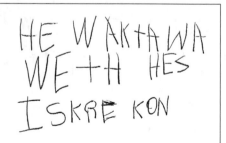

He walked away
with his
ice cream cone

And biked back
home and told
his friends about what
he had done
The
End

This is a real story! "Beg Brd Gos to Hav Fon Bikeing" has a beginning, a middle, and an end! Big Bird not only has fun biking, he gets the treat-of-all-treats, an ice cream cone, before heading home. Andrew has put himself in the story, too, as the "little boy standing nearby."

Now let's look more closely at Andrew's knowledge of both the conventions and the details of written language.

Book Conventions

- Andrew knows that there must be a title page. He has illustrated his.
- The story has shape. It opens dramatically, with Big Bird stepping out of the nest. He makes a decision to go biking, and even imagines what this will be like while he is getting dressed. He bikes in a crowd and sees an ice cream truck. Satisfied with his cone, he bikes back home and tells his friends about his adventures.
- The final picture shows Big Bird saying "BIE," and Andrew ends his story with THE END.

Literacy Knowledge

Andrew knows a lot about letters and their sounds. His writing is bold, and he uses clearly identifiable capital letters. Also, Andrew's attitude is bold; he doesn't stop the flow of his story to make sure each word is correct (an author's prerogative). Although his use of specific consonants and vowels may seem idiosyncratic to adult readers, they demonstrate logic ("vit" for "what") and a knowledge of where vowels are needed ("sad" for "said"). He also knows that:

- pages turn from right to left in the conventional manner.

- letters and words flow from left to right.

- lines of writing flow from the top to the bottom of the page.

- words are discrete entities that "live in their own spaces."

If you are asking yourself what the above analysis has to do with your child, remember that Andrew was nearly seven years old when he wrote this story. By knowing what to look for in Andrew's story, you'll be able to better observe and analyze everything your own child writes, no matter how simple or complex that writing may be.

PARENTS AS ROLE MODELS
Real-Life Reasons for Literacy

Your children observe you on a daily basis in real-life situations that demand a knowledge of reading and writing. They know what you are interested in, what you prefer to read, and what times of day you engage in reading and writing activities. They know if you like books or would rather read the newspaper and whether you spend a lot of time reading work-related material. And they will follow your lead. Now that you have this heavy burden on your shoulders, it will be a relief to know that you don't have to be a bookworm to encourage your child's literacy. You can be a storyteller, a list maker, a letter writer. As long as you demonstrate interest in some of the ingredients that make you a literate person, and as long as you encourage your child's literacy interests, you will be doing your job as a partner.

The following stories demonstrate how all parents, armed with determination and respect for learning, can encourage their children to read.

In 1976, a small but important study was published in England. A respected educational researcher, Dr. Margaret M. Clark, found the probable reasons for the spontaneous reading development of 32 Scottish children who were already reading with fluency and understanding at the time they entered kindergarten. These children came from a wide range of economic and educational backgrounds, from both large and small families, and they varied in terms of birth order within the family.

Clark found that the parents of these fluent readers were deeply involved in what interested their children and highly enthusiastic about education in general—even if they had not had much education themselves. Her vivid description of two families provides insight for all parents who wonder about how to build a positive reading atmosphere at home.

> One mother had left school at an early age, as had her husband; he had an unskilled job with long hours, while she also had an unskilled part-time job. Both, however, were avid readers and she described how on occasion they would sit absorbed in books and this seemed a shared social experience rather than the isolated activity it is sometimes considered. To quote, "We could be sitting for hours just reading."

> In a different family the mother, who was one of a large family, had left school at an early age as had the father, who was so bored that he had truanted frequently. Neither parent had followed any formal course of study after leaving school. The fluent reader in this family was the youngest of four children. For all, books formed a fascinating part of their life and a shared experience. On occasion the father would read to the children; he confessed he loved fairy stories himself. All six used the local library regularly and even on occasion read books selected by one of the others. Thus, here also, written and spoken language were experienced in a warm and accepting social context.

In a more recent study, entitled *Growing Up Literate*, Denny Taylor and Catherine Dorsey-Gaines studied emergent literacy among African-American children living in urban poverty who were seen by their parents as successfully learning to read and write. The authors watched these children spontaneously reading and writing in their home environments over a period of four years, collecting whatever written papers and drawings the children gave them. Taylor and Dorsey-Gaines also observed and analyzed the types of reading done by adult family members, uncovering a vast array of reasons and occasions for reading and writing that were necessary, informational, and recreational.

For the children, drawing, writing, and reading were closely connected; captions on pictures, cards, and letters provided frequent occasions to read. Despite uncertainty and hardship, despite a lack of resources, the families of these children were loving and supportive. They provided a rich oral tradition and opportunities to see adults reading in a variety of situations. These conditions produced a strong desire to read on the children's part and that desire both supported and enhanced their experience at school.

What this research underscores is that creating an inviting atmosphere in which children can learn to read can be accomplished by any parent, regardless of circumstance. How you go about becoming a partner in your child's reading process will be unique to your family's personal style.

5

Will My Child Have a Reading Problem?

And Other Special Circumstances

Countless times I've sat in my office and put my arm around a parent who was concerned about her child's reading progress. Because I have taught reading to children in the early grades, referred children for reading help, and worked closely with reading specialists, I know that there's no simple response.

My first task is to try to find out what the parent thinks the problem is. I have a great deal of respect for parents' instincts, but I'm also aware that anxiety about a child's initial reading progress can skew the parent's perception. Therefore, my next task is to try to sort out what's going on, and if necessary, recommend a specialist, who may take a number of approaches.

Some remedial reading programs assume that the most efficient strategy is to focus on building a firm foundation of letter sequences and letter/sound relationships, enabling the child to eventually break down—or decode—any word. Other approaches are more individual, taking into account the specific learning modes of each child. Brain research is expanding rapidly and may soon tell us more about the specific difficulties children may experience in learning to read.

At this point, take a deep breath! Remember that many children compensate, and will continue to compensate, for initial confusions as they set about the challenge of reading. Dr. Marie Clay, founder of the Reading Recovery program, which we'll look at later in this chapter, has said: "The confusion of young readers belongs to all beginners: It is just that successful children sort themselves out and the unsuccessful do not."

I have heard Courtney Cazden, an expert in the field of language and literacy, agree with Dr. Clay's position that one-tenth of a class of six-year-olds are likely to need extra help in reading. This means that two children in a class of 20, or three in a class of 30, may need sustained support. As I think back to my own years of teaching reading, these figures seem accurate.

Now take a second deep breath. Your child will learn to read! If you feel that extra help is needed, you can get it! It's available! You will need to think about the kind of extra help that is appropriate for your child, but the bottom line is that all children have the potential to become readers.

THINKING ABOUT YOUR CHILD
What to Look For

Observing your own child is both simpler and more confusing than watching a classroom of children. It's simpler because you are thinking about one child rather than 25; you can notice more and, of course, you know your child's style, personality, interests, and history. It can be confusing because your perspective is narrow—you're not seeing those 24 other children and the range of abilities that fall within a normal spectrum.

As a parent, you tend to be alert for potential problems because this is your child. If you are concerned about your child's reading progress, you can make some concrete observations that may help you evaluate what's going on. The following behaviors are common hitches in the learning-to-read process.

- Does your child reverse letters when he writes? Remember that this may simply be an immature stage of letter formation (like John, who reversed *b*'s and *d*'s until a second-grade classmate insisted on finding out what *bog* meant). Observe whether or not he confuses these letters when he's trying to read.

- Does your child write her words backward (from right to left: *saw* for *was*) or upside down? Make note of it if you're keeping a literacy journal. Also notice which words she does not reverse, and monitor her writing for general progress.

- Does your child show no interest in books? Observe carefully to determine if his interests lie elsewhere or if he seems to be avoiding all printed material. Turning pages, following lines of print from left to right, and eventually focusing on specific words and letters are all skills that beginning readers must eventually acquire, although the timing is unique for each individual child.

- Does your child have trouble expressing his thoughts in a logical sequence or get easily frustrated when trying to retrieve words, ideas, and events? Keep track of these instances to learn whether they occur once in a while or seem to be present as a general pattern.

Possible Problem Areas

If you are concerned about specific areas of your child's development that might impede literacy learning, consult first with your child's teacher and then check out your concerns with your child's pediatrician. Following are some specific problem areas and what you can do to address them:

Visual Acuity

If you suspect problems related to your child's visual acuity, your pediatrician will most probably suggest a checkup with an eye doctor. If something's amiss, there are many possible therapies, from eyeglasses to exercises, a good many of which are short-term and will involve some follow-through on your part at home. If the issue appears to be one of perception, involving sorting out or remembering visual images, you will want to follow up with a visit to a specialist in visual perception.

Hearing Difficulty

If you are concerned about your child's hearing or suspect he has trouble remembering what he hears, follow the familiar route of seeing your pediatrician first. Persistent ear infections or swollen adenoids may cause temporary hearing loss. A hearing loss of this kind may be at the root of auditory processing problems and, unless treated by a relatively simple surgical procedure, can be damaging to language development.

If part of your child's problem seems to be remembering what he hears, you can provide help by explaining an idea or sequence of events with pictures, such as illustrations of the afternoon's activities or a weekly visual calendar of events.

Muscular Weakness

Does your child shy away from holding a crayon or pencil, or find them difficult to control? You will want to have his doctor check for muscular weakness (as opposed to a developmental lag that falls within normal range). If necessary, an occupational therapist can achieve significant results.

Processing Difficulties

If your child demonstrates confusion in either expressing his thoughts or understanding what he hears, consider an evaluation by a person specifically trained in language development, disorders of speech and hearing, or learning disabilties. Once again, your pediatrician can refer you to the proper clinician. Should your child need professional help, the therapist will also suggest ways to help at home.

Teachers can assist children with processing difficulties by:

- supplying children with graphic organizers to help them organize their thinking.
- helping children to break information into chunks and then to focus on one chunk of information at a time.
- using technology to provide practice and motivation.

Listen to your own gut instincts. If reading difficulty is part of your family history, you will be particularly sensitive to possible problems and be on the lookout for potential red flags. If you feel that something's not quite right, share your thoughts with your child's teacher, the school psychologist, or an independent consultant. In every case, however, begin by looking at your child as objectively as possible—take into account what he can do, and balance this with your concerns.

How Schools Can Help

Traditional ways of helping children with reading problems include individual tutoring at home or at a reading specialist's office, and extra help in school, which may involve the child's leaving class to go to a separate room designated as a skills or learning center for an hour or so, usually between two and five times per week. A more recent trend is to have the school reading specialist come into the classroom and work with a small group of children there, which allows for more continuity and lessens disruption of the child's day.

Reading Recovery

Reading Recovery is a program developed by Dr. Marie Clay, of the University of Auckland, and originally used in the schools of New Zealand to detect and correct reading difficulty. The basic premise is that children's reading behaviors should be evaluated at age six in order to identify those children most in need of an intense intervention program.

Evaluators look first at what the child knows about a book and its contents, and check for knowledge of separate words, letter identification, directionality, and ability to use picture clues for story sense. Then they assess the child's ability to hear and write down letter sounds. Throughout the procedure, they highlight and praise what the child already knows. Finally, they share their findings with the child's parents and teacher.

Each Reading Recovery session follows a consistent routine:

- The child and teacher examine and read a selection of books together.

- The child reads the previous day's book to the teacher. At the same time, the teacher keeps a "running record," noting accuracy and analyzing errors.

- The teacher tailors exercises to the child's individual needs, to strengthen letter identification and vocabulary recognition.

- The teacher helps the child to write a sentence or short paragraph of a new story or one already in progress, perhaps writing down the child's dictated words or the letters she hears, and filling in missing letters where appropriate. A sentence strip is made from one of the sentences, then cut up into separate words that the child can shuffle and put back in order.

- Finally, the teacher introduces a new book, and child and teacher examine it together. This may be an unfamiliar book, to draw the child's attention to the print, or a book with familiar text, to build the child's confidence. Pictures are discussed as clues to the meaning of the story.

Reading Recovery teachers lavish praise throughout the sessions. They encourage children to point to each word and to check back to previous words, sentences, or pages to identify a particular word or confirm a story understanding. Reading Recovery has a high success rate; however, not every school offers this program as it requires the participation of a highly trained Reading Recovery teacher.

Other classroom intervention strategies include using paired reading, in which a more fluent and less fluent reader work together; providing magnet or felt boards for children who benefit from a multisensory, hands-on approach; and offering technology programs to help children gain extra practice in reading and skills development.

If English Is a Second Language

If yours is a home where a language other than English is spoken, your child can have the advantage of growing up to be fluent in two languages. He will also have the gifts of your cultural traditions and family lore that illuminate the power of language and story, both spoken and written. Children who speak two languages can, in fact, be highly successful in school.

I will always remember one particular class of children whom I taught for two consecutive years, both as first- and second-graders. This class included a larger than usual number (for my school district) of children for whom English was—or was to become in my classroom—a second language. There were several Spanish-speaking children with limited English proficiency, two Japanese children who spoke no English at all, a child of Greek background, and one of Romanian background, all of whom spoke their native languages at home, as well as children of Polish and Israeli descent. In the middle of first grade, a new child from Germany joined us who spoke no English at all.

My school had an ESL (English as a Second Language) program that removed children classified as needing English-language remediation from the classroom twice a week, for one half hour at a time. Because of their limited time together, the ESL teacher concentrated with the children on specific tasks such as working on ditto sheets and learning the names of familiar objects. Although these sessions were helpful, it was clear that the children could benefit from classroom activities and discussions, which would give them practice with the structure of spoken English.

Our class had rich resources in the parents who generously shared their cultural traditions with us: Maria's family taught us Mexican songs, Lola's father helped the children prepare a Greek meal, Yuki's mother helped us celebrate Japanese Boy's Day, Andrew's grandmother taught us Polish dances. Although I myself possessed no special ESL skills, the non-English-speaking children progressed remarkably well in learning to communicate with their peers. As we always made time for discussion, reading aloud, and plenty of interaction around activities, I saw that the native English-speaking children were able to interpret words and phrases—often through gesture—in a natural and effective way, as they made friends with their non-English-speaking classmates.

Gradually all the children were able to converse with each other... and they began to read and write. Some of the linguistically diverse children spoke and wrote with a simpler vocabulary, but they showed clear and consistent progress. Of course, some were more temperamentally shy and others more outgoing, and that influenced the frequency and persistence with which they used English.

Manfred, the German youngster who entered mid-year, had a very difficult time at first. He didn't want to say anything if he couldn't say it right! This trait, along with the problem of being new to a group of children already cohesive and comfortable together by the time he arrived, made him angry and resistant. Still, by the end of first grade he demonstrated remarkable progress: His good athletic skills gave him confidence, he had made a few friends, and he could converse in two- or three-word sentences. If I had been clairvoyant, I would have been able to see him striding across the stage and declaring his lines with gusto as The Giant in our second-grade class play.

According to figures reported by state education departments and experts in the field of limited English proficiency (sometimes referred to as LEP), between 2 million and 3.5 million students in this country are classified as linguistically diverse. These figures do not include children from diverse backgrounds who are proficient in English. When analyzed according to percentages, the statistics break down as 75% Spanish-speaking, 12% speakers of Asian languages, and 10% speakers of Native American, European, and Arabic languages. These children are served in public schools through a variety of programs including bilingual education and ESL, programs that are important and supportive of the efforts of parents and classroom teachers.

The summer between first and second grade, I picked up C. S. Lewis's *The Lion, the Witch, and the Wardrobe* and was hooked after two pages. I could "taste" the way it would feel to read this book aloud to the children I already knew so well. Although my colleagues assured me that this story was more appropriate for fourth-graders and, more forcefully, told me that I was crazy to try to read it to a group of children from such diverse language backgrounds, I couldn't give it up. There was some pretty heavy content, but I felt…I hoped…we could handle it together.

The following spring, as I turned to the last page of Lewis's book and read the final words aloud, my class sat in total silence…then erupted. It just couldn't be over! They insisted on writing about it, on drawing and painting about it, and finally convinced me that they must put on a play based on the book. They decided that they would structure the play themselves, make the scenery and sew the costumes in the art room, in class, at home! And indeed they did all of this, performing the play movingly for their parents and for other classes in the school.

In doing research for this book, I was surprised and gratified to discover that what I learned in the classroom as a teacher almost 20 years ago is now supported by much of the current literature concerning children for whom English is a second language. Although there is controversy about which language should be the child's primary avenue to literacy, educators increasingly agree that children coming to literacy through their second language should be taught in ways that are meaningful and relevant to them: at home, in classrooms, and within special school programs.

The following precepts are helpful guides not only for teachers but also for parents whose children are in the process of learning English.

Children need not be fluent in English in order to hear stories read aloud or to begin to write and read in their second language. My second-grade children's rapt attention, at every stage of hearing *The Lion, the Witch, and the Wardrobe* read aloud, resulted in their own desire to talk about the play and perform it, and in their zeal to make up further stories about the characters and write about them.

Children need to feel good about themselves, and to make friends, as they risk the inevitable errors of inflection, grammar, and word selection that are all part of learning a new language. For example, Manfred, the child who entered my class without speaking or understanding a single word of English, needed first to trust his classmates before assuming a role in our class play. With a confidence born of friendship, he was then able to make up his own dialogue in a creative-dramatics production.

Children who are learning English as a second language benefit from hearing the natural flow of English in a variety of situations. Yuki and Lola, the Japanese and Greek children who played "trees" in the play, had no lines but were exposed to the rich words connected with all aspects of putting on our drama. Quiet, well-behaved children, they were as enthusiastic as the most obstreperous, and their spoken and written language showed tremendous growth by the end of the year.

Children benefit from practicing English at home as well as in school. If English is also your second language, set aside an "English only" time for conversation. Your child will model your enthusiasm as a learner.

The richness that our country derives from the families of different ethnicities and cultures who make up our society is a cause for celebration. When children enter school, special programs combine with classroom experiences to provide substantial help as they encounter the challenges of learning to speak, to write, and to read in their new language. As your child learns to speak English with neighborhood friends and at school, you can encourage his progress, while still treasuring your native language, traditions, and stories.

CHAPTER

6

You and Your Child's School
Working Together

I n my years of work with families and schools, children have been among my most powerful informants. They have taught me to respect their intuitive understanding of relationships. They have demonstrated an uncanny ability to know when their parents and teachers are really talking, and often what they are talking about! And although they may not verbally express their thoughts, children's behavior invariably reflects a sense of relief when the adults who care for and spend the most time with them are working as a team. Feelings of relief are followed by confidence, a confidence that comes from children knowing that those they love are communicating with each other.

Nursery schools and child-care centers allow for parent-teacher communication and set aside some significant time at points during the year for conferencing. In settings where children spend large portions of the day, there may be weekly or even daily opportunities, however brief, for parents and teachers to connect.

OPENING AVENUES OF COMMUNICATION

When your child enters elementary school, a new phase of life begins for both of you. The move from child-care center, nursery school, or home brings a different set of challenges. Your child will now be in a larger setting, often for a longer day, and will interact with a variety of adults—especially if the school has a range of special-area programs such as music, art, physical education, and library time. This can feel like you are "turning over" or "giving up" your child to an unknown world. In this new culture, your most immediate and important contact is the classroom teacher.

One recent September, a young mother whose son had attended my early childhood center asked to see me. Douglas had recently started first grade at their local public school, and she was very upset. Ten days before, Douglas had come home with a "frown face" on his homework sheet and the words "Please do this over." Shortly afterward, he began saying he didn't want to go to school, and his mom was pretty sure the frown face was the cause of the problem. Douglas was sensitive and could easily be discouraged. Still, Ms. Halpern was supposed to be the best first-grade teacher, and Mom didn't want to sound like a complainer or to "have Ms. Halpern take it wrong and get mad at Douglas."

This story highlights some of the conflicting feelings aroused in parents when young children enter the larger world of the elementary school. It also suggests some basic choices faced by the adults in question:

- How can a parent become an active participant in a child's school environment?
- When is it important to express concerns? How can a parent approach a teacher outside of the formal conference setting?
- How can a parent use formal conferencing as a dialogue through which both the parent and teacher share information about the child's progress and strengths?

In Douglas's case, his mother and teacher came together to help each other make the child they shared feel successful. Mom met with Ms. Halpern, telling her how sensitive he was and that he might have construed the comments on his homework sheet as criticism. Ms. Halpern was appreciative of the information and had a talk with Douglas about the many things he was doing successfully. By October 1, Douglas was back to bounding through the door of the school. His mom had successfully bridged the transition between a smaller preschool setting and a big elementary school. She opted for direct communication and found a way to join in a partnership with Doug's teacher.

Often, there is some confusion as families move from the communication practices of smaller settings to the necessarily different culture of the elementary school. Adding to the confusion is the larger issue of academics, particularly the question of how and when your child will become an independent reader.

UNDERSTANDING YOUR SCHOOL'S READING PROGRAM

Schools use different approaches in the teaching of reading, which are adapted by the teacher to fit the needs of the children in her classroom. The best information we have to date about children learning to read in school indicates that reading competencies evolve most successfully in the context of a balanced literacy program. In this chapter we'll clarify terms and review reading approaches that have played a part in the evolution of current thinking about the teaching of reading.

Phonics

Phonics is the relationship between sounds in speech and spelling patterns in print. A phonics approach to reading advocates building up or breaking down a written word into separate sounds, a strategy that is often referred to as decoding. It assumes that children must first learn to connect separate spoken sounds, called phonemes, with their corresponding written letters and letter combinations, called graphemes. They then must learn to link the graphemes together as a way of analyzing, or decoding, whole words.

Christi, whom we met in Chapter 1 and who passionately loved letters and their sounds, would have reveled in the systematic nature of a reading program that stressed phonics. She would have thought it logical to learn the sounds of letters first, then blend them into words, and finally into sentences. Although the blending aspect was difficult for Christi and meaning "clicked in" long after she was able to decode separate words, phonics was her preferred reading strategy initially.

Children need to be able to recognize the sound-symbol relationship between speech and print, automatically, to read fluently. For some children, guided practice in unraveling these relationships is the first step toward understanding the meaning of the printed word.

Sight Words

Sylvia Ashton-Warner's work with Maori children in New Zealand highlights the key features of the sight word method. This method is based on the belief that children can learn to read words by taking visual note of their length and shape. Ashton-Warner developed a method, which she called the "key vocabulary," in mixed-race classrooms of white and Maori (Aborigine) children in her native New Zealand in the 1950s.

Observing that Maori children appeared to have more difficulty than their white classmates with beginning reading, she determined that the methods and materials of the "infant school" (as British, Australian, and New Zealand early childhood classrooms are called) were inappropriately geared to the white culture. Her solution was to ask each child to tell her a word that meant something important to him each day. She wrote this word on a card, which in turn became the child's possession. Ashton-Warner noticed that really meaningful words were handled, examined...and remembered! The meaningful words could then be formed into sentences and used as a basis for beginning writing.

Ashton-Warner used her method successfully in racially diverse classrooms for many years. Her book, *Teacher*, is a classic in the education field. Many American educators today use individual word-card collections with their children as a way to use sight words in a meaningful context.

Guided Reading

In a guided reading group, a small group of children read a piece of text with the teacher. A classroom in which guided reading is practiced requires several sets of books at different reading levels, so that children can be matched to the appropriate text. The text is considered appropriate if a child can read most, but not all, of it fluently. Teachers also try to make matches based on interest.

The teacher's role in a guided-reading lesson is to help children through trouble spots in the stories by encouraging them to use reading strategies such as context clues, language clues, and phonics. Guided-reading lessons focus on skills development within the context of an enjoyable shared-reading experience.

Whole Language

There have always been advocates for a child's right to learn to read at school in a natural way, making use of his own interests, intuitions, and personal reading timetable. Many years ago I was fortunate enough to meet and hear a lecture by one of the great "teacher of teachers," Leland Jacobs, who at that time was in his 80s and professor emeritus at Columbia University's Teachers College. He spoke with passion and insight about the power of literature to lure children into reading. He believed that teachers must provide beginning readers with books of all kinds and levels of difficulty: picture books, storybooks, books on every possible topic that might connect with children's interests. He believed that teachers should spend time reading books to children on a daily basis, that they should show their own enthusiasm for books, and that they should provide children with time to browse in a classroom library and read to and with each other.

A whole language approach incorporates the belief that children's early reading and writing are closely connected, best fostered in a meaningful context, and interwoven into all aspects of curriculum. It celebrates the power of literature. While acknowledging the importance of phonemic awareness, the whole language approach de-emphasizes the teaching of phonics as the first step to reading.

American educators have absorbed whole language influences from many sources. New Zealand is most often credited as the birthplace of whole language, and Big Books—books that are big enough to be seen by a whole class—are one of its most visible tools. Authentic Big Books have certain unmistakable characteristics: They are, first and foremost, good literature; their text is limited but predictable (rhyming or containing predictable phrases); and they are large enough in both illustration and text to engage an entire group of children in the reading experience.

Major American contributors to the whole language approach include, among many others, Donald Graves, of the University of New Hampshire, and Lucy M. Calkins, of Teachers College, Columbia University, both of whom have carried out extensive analysis of children's writing process. Their research has focused on what happens when children are encouraged to write using their own inventive or invented spelling. Given ample opportunities for writing and sharing their work, along with editing help from their peers and teachers, children eventually refine their spelling as they gain phonic insights. The writing process approach is often incorporated into a whole language classroom because it honors children's efforts to figure out the nature of print and fosters the spontaneous development of competent readers and writers.

Balanced Literacy

Increasingly, educators are moving toward combining both skills-based and literature-based elements in approaching the teaching of reading through a balanced literacy program. According to a recent issue of The Harvard Education Letter, "Scholars...have begun to call for consensus on the balanced approach." In his new book, *Teaching Our Children to Read*, Bill Honig, former commissioner of education for California, says that both a literature-driven and language-rich reading program and a comprehensive, organized skills development program are essential.

As we think about the teaching of literacy, it seems logical, given children's variations in learning pace and approaches to print, that teachers use a wide net to engage their interests through real-life experiences, books, and writing opportunities, as well as targeted strategies to help each child progress to his or her fullest potential.

Teachers who embrace a balanced approach go beyond single methods to take note of each child's learning behaviors. In a balanced literacy program, the teacher carefully observes and documents children's literacy learning, enabling her to work effectively with each child and her class as a whole.

Assessment Strategies

The goal of assessment is to find out what's needed and to provide support by keeping track of each child's progress, thus reducing the need for prolonged remedial help. Teachers use a range of assessment tools, both formal and informal, that actively involve parents in their children's learning while gauging each child's progress along a continuum.

The typical range of assessment tools includes traditional pen and paper assessment, collections of writing samples, and one-on-one interviews with children. The Primary Language Record and Portfolio Assessment are two strategies that can be used to actively involve the parent in a child's reading development.

The Primary Language Record

The Primary Language Record is a one-on-one assessment tool that provides detailed records of a child's literacy development.

Picture a classroom outfitted with books of all kinds and a teacher head-to-head with one child as they read together amid a swarm of busy youngsters. Hear the hum of children reading to each other, and aloud to themselves; see others reading silently, wrapped in the world of self-selected books. To the casual passerby, this scene may look like a "reading free-for-all" but in this classroom, fluent readers are helping others with less facility, and even children who cannot yet read are considered part of the reading community.

How can one teacher know what's really going on with each child in a classroom like the above? As the children read, write, and converse, the teacher takes careful notes in one-on-one encounters with individual students. These notes are part of the Primary Language Record, a carefully structured assessment and reporting tool that helps teachers record children's strengths, allows for the development of plans to support weaker areas of understanding, and provides in-depth knowledge to share with parents about their children's literacy development.

Portfolio Assessment

Portfolios of children's work have been used as assessment tools by early childhood teachers for decades, but the concept of portfolios has only recently gained acceptance by some state education departments and school districts.

Looking at collections of children's paintings, drawings, writing, audio recordings, and the teacher's anecdotal records over a six-month or school-year period can give a powerful picture of children's abilities and help parents and teachers better assess reading progress. You, too, can keep a home-based portfolio of your child's work. Use the portfolio for enjoyment and insight into your child's progress over time. If you are keeping a literacy journal, you are already on your way!

TAKING A ROLE IN YOUR CHILD'S FORMAL EDUCATION

The first questions to ask yourself are "Do I understand my school's philosophy of education?" and "How is the philosophy demonstrated in the way my child is being taught to read?" These are big questions, which will require you to pull together as much information as you can.

Gathering the Information

Your first step will be to peruse all available material published by your school concerning the educational approach and curriculum. This information can usually be found in PTA handbooks, school-generated handbooks designed to acquaint you with the school's educational philosophy and expectations, and grade-level curriculum guidelines. Here are some more ways you can add to your information:

- Informally observe the classroom as you leave or pick up your child at school. What kinds of books and other reading materials do you see? Does the classroom have a library corner where children can browse? Are there sets of basal readers on the shelves? Is there evidence of children's dictated stories or their own writings?

- Listen carefully and ask questions on "Back to School" night as you seek to understand the teacher's reading program. Teachers have much to deal with on these evenings, so if you feel your questions haven't been answered fully, be sure to follow them up at some other time.

- Most important, establish a comfortable relationship with the teacher, seeking ways to communicate that fit her style, whether it be by telephone, to-and-from-school notes, or personal conferences. You may not endorse everything that happens in the classroom, but putting the mechanisms in place for effective parent-teacher communication will ultimately benefit your child. Also keep in mind that it's perfectly appropriate to seek the principal's advice and to ask for confidentiality, or to request a meeting with both principal and teacher, should the going get tough.

Using the Information

If you've followed the above guidelines, at this point you will have a basic understanding of both the school's and the teacher's approach to teaching reading, and some open avenues for communication.

Whatever our differences, we can be sure that parent-school collaboration produces more positive attitudes in students and parents, and increased self-esteem in teachers. Of course, that's easier said than done. But if you have "done your homework"—spent time observing your child's emerging literacy and done your own research to find out about your school's programs—then you will be able to engage in the kind of productive dialogue that leads to collaboration. If true collaboration is to develop, however, a set of conditions needs to be in place:

■ **Condition 1:** Schools are eager for children's success and parents' satisfaction.

■ **Condition 2:** Teachers care about the children they teach and work hard to help them learn.

■ **Condition 3:** Parents know more about their individual children than anyone else does.

If everyone involved accepts these conditions, then you will all be able to work together for the child's benefit, despite possible disagreements in belief and approach.

WORKING TOGETHER

Knowing that parents and teachers are working together is tremendously important for children. It implies that the adults in their lives are supportive, that they have expectations, and that these expectations are consistent.

Working Together for the Child

In Chapter 1 we considered a little girl named Kathryn who adored books, but who had some initial difficulty learning to read them. A closer look at what might have been a sticky situation between Kathryn's parents and her teacher gives us a specific example of what "working together" is all about.

Susan, Kathryn's teacher, was a seasoned learning-disabilities specialist, but new to a first-grade classroom. Her assessment of Kathryn's reading development was that something was definitely wrong, that Kathryn most probably had a learning disability. Walter and Maria, Kathryn's parents, disagreed. They saw their daughter as a highly sensitive child, coping with the life event of a new sibling and becoming a reader at her own pace.

Susan, who invited parents into her room on a regular basis, welcomed Walter's help once a week as a reading tutor. Despite some disagreement between them about approaches to reading instruction, parents and teacher eventually determined that an evaluation by the school psychologist was an acceptable next step for Kathryn.

Test results showed Kathryn to be highly verbal but weak in visual areas of matching letters and words. The test scores, however, did not indicate a need for special help. At this point, Maria and Walter decided to seek the advice of a pediatric optometrist, who diagnosed Kathryn with a rare but easily correctable form of visual impairment. Treatment brought quick results, and Kathryn is now racing ahead in her reading ability.

This brief story allows us to see how working together with your child's school can be successful, provided the necessary conditions exist:

- **Condition 1:** The School. Kathryn was placed with Susan by the school administration because of her experience with "late" readers.

- **Condition 2:** The Teacher. Susan invited Kathryn's parents into her room on a regular basis, spoke with them by phone, and met with them in conferences.

- **Condition 3:** The Parents. Kathryn's parents made persistent efforts to explain their daughter's personality to both the teacher and the school psychologist, urging a more relaxed approach to reading instruction.

Despite their differences, all the adults involved maintained mutual respect. The results included a meeting of personal and professional insights on the adults' part, and most important, a happy child who feels good about herself and loves her teacher.

Working Together for the School

Parents can play major roles in schools in several important ways. Many fathers or mothers become the parent representative for their child's class. Your school undoubtedly has a Parent Teacher Association (PTA) that has a number of committees on which you can serve. As a member of the PTA, you will get to know teachers better and learn more about how your school operates.

In some states (New York, for example), site-based management teams have been mandated. These teams, composed of parents, teachers, and administrators, are charged with the major task of evaluating their schools' curricula and making long-range plans for school improvement. If your state education department has such a plan, you can find out how teams are selected and how you might put your name forward in your own school.

When school meetings are called or speakers presented, try to attend, no matter how hectic your schedule may be. You'll learn more about the school's educational philosophy, and your child will see that you view her education as a priority. Because many adults work outside the home, meetings are often held at night to encourage both working mothers and fathers to attend. (If no evening meetings are scheduled, lobby for them!)

And don't forget the school board elections. Yes, of course you should study the issues and vote. But remember that every parent is a potential school board member, and you can be one too. (At a recent local school board meeting, I was stunned to see that four of my former early child-hood center parents were members.) It is a powerful way to work with others for the excellence of your school and the education of your child.

You can help make your child's education a success by remembering that you are an important partner in the process.

This book has tried to open a window on how children become read-ers. I hope I have empowered you with the knowledge that, through observation, you can know better than anyone else how your child is likely to enter the reading community. In this way, you will be able to facilitate your child's success in school.

It would have been easier if I'd said, "This is how all children learn to read, and this is what you should do!" But because there is no single recipe, it would not have been truthful. Instead, I remind you that your child *will* learn to read, and I leave you with a set of challenges:

- Trust yourself and your own powers of observation.
- Support your child's unique approach to solving the riddles of reading.
- Share your knowledge with teachers.
- Listen to the insights teachers may have for you.
- Maintain confidence if the road gets rocky.
- And above all, enjoy the ride!

Afterword

Reflecting on Your Child as a Learner

When we use the word *literate* today, we are conscious that its meaning is wider than at any time in our history. Arnold Packer, a researcher at Johns Hopkins University, envisions a broad definition of literacy:

> Literacy is the ability to process information for a purpose. One purpose is to derive pleasure, to know how to read a story and get emotional satisfaction from it. A second purpose is to read for information in order to form a reasoned opinion or make a sound decision. A third purpose is to be able to apply what we know and take action, to produce new things.

Literacy is a big idea, encompassing the fact that reading develops as an ongoing process. How can parents use this expanded concept of literacy as their children are learning to read and write? Instead of judging how and when children learn to read as "intelligence barometers," or seeing your child's pace and approach to reading as indicative of his ability to learn, you can view literacy in the wider context of learning.

The following ideas, supported by both theory and practice, can help you to relax as your child's literacy learning unfolds:

Your child's dispositions and feelings join with knowledge and skills to keep her open to learning opportunities of all kinds.

We all know that when kids feel good about themselves, they are not only more fun to be with, they are more enthusiastic and open to learning. We don't, however, always give equal weight to the importance of dispositions and feelings in young children's learning.

Eminent author and educator Lilian Katz suggests that children's motivation to learn is an accepted "given." After all, children learn to crawl, to walk, and to speak not only by modeling their behavior on others', but through practice that is naturally motivated. This motivation to discover, and each child's specific propensity for exuberance, thoughtfulness, empathy, or generosity, can be thought of as habits of mind that are strengthened by the acknowledgment of others. Resultant feelings of self-confidence and belonging will then support the more cognitive, or intellectual, strands of skills and knowledge. On the flip side, if feelings are ignored, a sense of incompetence or rejection may result. Katz asks that we see temperament, positive interactions, and informal pleasures as pillars that serve not only as strong supports for children's academic understanding, but as independent areas of learning that influence the achievement of academic success.

Children of all dispositions are engaged learners from birth and have "a hundred languages" through which to express themselves.

Children have unlimited modes of expression, as long as we provide them with materials and opportunities to explore. This is the meaning of "the hundred languages of children," an expression from the early childhood schools of Reggio Emilia, Italy. Educators there see children as strong, capable, and ambitious from birth. Close observation of young children reveals their perseverance in tracking a worm on the ground, chasing a tantalizing butterfly, or insisting on hearing the same story again and again.

Those who have visited the Reggio schools or exhibits come away breathless at children's accomplishments, especially the conceptual ideas they are able to express through their multidimensional artwork. Working together in small groups on topics of interest to them, four-, five-, and six-year-olds construct an elaborately intricate "amusement park for birds," create murals of great beauty and detail, investigate the properties of rain, shadows, or other natural phenomena, and devise and organize a schoolwide "long jump" contest. Into these investigations are woven the "basic skills" of reading, writing, and computing, present because they are the means of expression for the projects underway.

Your child's intelligence is not simply measured by reading and writing facility; he can be endowed with a number of multiple intelligences.

Consider the phenomenal thinking of musicians, dancers, athletes, architects, visual artists, scientists, and statesmen. Whether you are using your body skillfully, creating a work of art or a scientific invention, or weighing the implications of a big decision, your mind is actively engaged in the process.

Howard Gardner, a psychologist and learning theorist at Harvard University, has conceptualized a theory of multiple intelligences. The exciting implications of Gardner's theory allow us to value thinking of different kinds as both legitimate and sometimes brilliant. He has identified the following seven core intelligences, and he is in the process of conducting work on others:

- **Linguistic Intelligence**: demonstrated by either the very verbal, and/or those for whom reading and writing come easily, such as writers, editors, and journalists.

- **Logical-Mathemetical Intelligence**: demonstrated by those who show facility in working with numbers, a strong capacity for deductive reasoning, abstract thinking, and the ability to see patterns. These traits are often seen in scientists, computer programmers, and engineers.

- **Spatial Intelligence**: demonstrated by artists, architects, designers, and others with the ability to have an idea, visualize it as a mental image, and then construct it in a spatial form.

- **Bodily-Kinesthetic Intelligence**: athletic and aesthetic prowess, as demonstrated by athletes or physical artists (the gymnast, dancer, skater) who illustrate the intelligence of the body at work.

- **Musical Intelligence**: exhibited by those who are drawn to music and demonstrate the thought processes that underlie the ability to perform or compose.

- **Interpersonal Intelligence**: interpersonal gifts, a sense of what will work and with whom, demonstrated by those with leadership qualities and an intuitive understanding of others.

- **Intrapersonal Intelligence**: demonstrated by those with strong powers of reflection, observers who digest what's going on in their environments while processing events — qualities that often result in careers in psychology, philosophy, and writing.

As you watch your child engaging in and enjoying different kinds of activities, including those considered academic, athletic, artistic, or people-oriented, you can be sure that his mind is at work and that he is demonstrating literacy in the broadest sense of the word.

Literacy is connected to life.

Projects and ideas that engage your child while encouraging thinking and discussion result in rich opportunities for literacy learning.

Have you ever worried that a family trip to the zoo or museum, a picnic on the beach or at a nature preserve, or simply a walk to your local park might be time better spent on academic pursuits? If so, have no fear! Throughout history, scholars of education and good observers of children have noted the role of experience in learning.

In their book *Engaging Children's Minds*, Lilian Katz and Sylvia Chard build on the thought and work of John Dewey to describe the Project Approach, a way of using classroom projects, trips, and experiences to allow for children's active participation in their own studies. In the Project Approach, thoughtfully structured projects are centered on topics of interest to children and emphasize interaction with people, objects, and environments.

To give you a peek at the process, picture the following scenario described by the authors:

> [A] small group of children were working together on a picture of an ambulance. They wanted to display it with strings running from different parts of the vehicle to word labels around the outside of the picture. Two children wrote the labels, one measured and cut suitable lengths of string, and another pinned the strings in place. The child who pinned the strings would have had great difficulty writing the labels, but his contribution was valued because he performed a necessary task. At the same time, he improved his reading ability while matching the words and objects.

Every time you include your own child in planning and participation, supply materials and avenues for self-expression, engage in conversation, and create a record of the experiences you share, you are opening windows of literacy and learning. You are building strength in your child to take on the challenges that await us all in the twenty-first century.

Frequently Asked Questions

. . . and Answers

Q. *When will my child learn to read?*

A. Experts tell us that children most often learn to read independently between the ages of five and seven. Just as in learning to talk, learning to read is a process that will unfold over time. Look for the preliminary signs of reading, such as recognizing occasional letters and words, experimenting with writing, looking at books, and turning pages.

Q. *My daughter is four years old and loves to be read to, but she has little interest in looking at books on her own. Should I be worried?*

A. As long as she enjoys having you read to her, you can be sure that books hold interest for your child. In fact, getting pleasure from listening to others read is considered an important step in the process of learning to read. Your daughter already sees you as a reading model, so keep up the good work!

Q. *My four-year-old knows all her letters! Is she "gifted"?*

A. All children have areas of "giftedness," and some love to play with letters and their sounds. Remember that memorizing the alphabet is not the same thing as recognizing and naming each letter, and that further steps will require knowing all the sounds of the letters, as well as blending the sounds into words.

Q. *I thought that kindergarten was the beginning of "real school," but the teacher tells me my child spends a lot of time playing in the classroom. She seems to think this is okay, but I want my son to understand the meaning of real work. What should I do?*

A. Dramatic play—sometimes called "symbolic play"—is work for five-year-olds. The effort and planning your child invests in creating pretend dramas, whether with blocks, in a pretend play corner, or on the playground, means that he has learned to substitute one set of props and ideas for another. This kind of play is important for all children. It not only creates a basis for understanding the abstract nature of letters and words, but its symbolic nature can translate to other areas of learning as well.

Q. *Should I expect my child to learn to read in kindergarten?*

A. By the time a child reaches kindergarten, she may have acquired enough skills to read independently. However, it is more common that children this age are not at this level. Instead of expecting your child to read, watch for the development of early reading behaviors. These include looking at books for pleasure, using the pictures to help tell the story of a book in your child's own words, and recognizing signs, labels, and at least some letters of the alphabet.

Q. *My five-year-old doesn't recognize any of his letters. Should I panic?*

A. Children learn to read in different ways, and some recognize whole words more easily than their parts. However, knowing letters and their sounds is an important reading insight. Talk to your child's teacher about strategies to use at home, such as playing with letter magnets or baking letter pretzels. Your child's name is a great place to start letter learning!

Q. *My child is starting first grade, and she's worried that she won't learn to read. What can I do to reassure her?*

A. Most children start to read independently sometime during first grade, though in some cases it happens later. Assure your child that her teacher is there to help her. You can assist by sharing books at home, encouraging her reading and writing efforts, and helping her feel confident in her abilities. When the time is right, she'll read on her own!

Q. *My first-grader is six and a half and he still can't read on his own. His father and I both had trouble with reading in school, and we're desperately worried that he's going to have the same kinds of problems. Are we overreacting?*

A. Not necessarily. Have a conference with his teacher and share your concerns, then try to balance her views with your own. Your child may be developing reading strategies in school that he's not demonstrating at home, or perhaps he's one of those children who make a giant leap between first and second grade. On the other hand, if the teacher is concerned as well, some form of assessment may be helpful.

Q. *Is it okay for my beginning reader to point to each word with her finger?*

A. Using your finger to keep track of the words you're reading is a very efficient tactic! It helps a reader to focus on a specific word without impeding the meaning. Admire your youngster's concentration, and have faith that finger-pointing will fade as fluency increases.

Q. *My child has memorized several books, but I know he's not really reading. How should I handle this?*

A. Memorizing the words that go with the pictures in a book is an important step in learning to read. It's a logical progression to memorize the spoken words, then make connections between spoken words and the words that are written under the pictures or on the opposite page.

Q. *Why is reading aloud to my child important?*

A. Reading aloud can inspire children of all ages to enter the world of literacy. The closeness you experience when reading aloud helps to enhance your child's self-esteem, creates a positive connection to books, and provides motivation to discover the content between the covers.

Q. *How do I know which books to choose for my child?*

A. Offer your child a variety of books. Choose books to read aloud, picture books and easy readers, and books with repeated words, lines, or phrases that encourage your child to "read along." Think about your child's special interests as you make your choices. If your child is already reading, err on the easy side in terms of vocabulary and sentence structure to encourage success. Add children's books designated as classics by your local library or bookstore, and any others that you particularly love.

Q. *If my child is starting to read to himself, shouldn't I stop reading to him?*

A. No. You're never too old to be read to! Children who read early will deeply regret the absence of the "being read to" experience if it's taken away.

Books for Parents

Ashton-Warner, Sylvia. *Teacher*. Simon & Schuster, 1963.

Bettelheim, Bruno and Zelan, Karen. *On Learning to Read: The Child's Fascination With Meaning*. Vintage Books, 1982.

Bialostok, Steven. *Raising Readers: Helping Your Child to Literacy*. Peguis Publishers, 1992.

Boegehold, Betty D. *Getting Ready to Read*. Ballantine Books, 1984.

Butler, Dorothy and Clay, Marie. *Reading Begins at Home*. Heinemann, 1983.

Clay, Marie M. *Writing Begins at Home*. Heinemann, 1987.
———. *What Did I Write?: Beginning Writing Behavior*. Heinemann, 1984.

Cullinan, Bernice E. *Read to Me: Raising Kids Who Love to Read*. Scholastic, 1992.

Kropp, Paul. *Raising a Reader*. Doubleday, 1984.

Rosenthal, Nadine. *Speaking of Reading*. Heinemann, 1995.

Schickedanz, Judith A. *More Than the ABCs: The Early Stages of Reading and Writing*. National Association for the Education of Young Children, 1986.

Smith, Frank. *Reading Without Nonsense*. Teachers College Press, 1979.

Trelease, Jim. *The Read-Aloud Handbook*. Penguin Books, 1985.

Weaver, Constance. *Understanding Whole Language: From Principles to Practice*. Heinemann, 1990.

Books for Young Readers and Readers-to-Be

Ahlberg, Janet and Allan. *Peek-a-Boo!* Viking Press, 1981.

Bang, Molly. *Ten, Nine, Eight*. Greenwillow Books, 1983.

Brown, Marc. *Hand Rhymes*. E. P. Dutton, 1985.

Brown, Margaret Wise. *Goodnight Moon*. Harper, 1947.
———. *The Runaway Bunny*. Harper, 1942.

Capucilli, Alyssa. *Inside a Barn in the Country*. Scholastic Inc., 1993.

Carle, Eric. *Do You Want to Be My Friend?* Crowell, 1981.
————. *Have You Seen My Cat?* F. Watts, 1973.

Doyle, Charlotte. *Freddie's Spaghetti.* Random House, 1991.

Ehlert, Lois. *Feathers for Lunch.* Harcourt Brace Jovanovich, 1990.

Ga'g, Wanda. *Millions of Cats.* Coward McCann, 1928.

Galdone, Paul. *The Gingerbread Boy.* Seabury Press, 1975.
————. *The Little Red Hen.* Scholastic Inc., 1973.
————. *The Three Bears.* Clarion Books, 1972.
————. *The Three Billy Goats Gruff.* Seabury Press, 1973.

Guarino, Deborah. *Is Your Mama a Llama?* Scholastic Inc., 1989.

Hoberman, Mary Ann. *A House Is a House for Me.* Viking Press, 1978.

Kraus, Robert. *Come Out and Play, Little Mouse.* Greenwillow Books, 1987.

Martin, Bill, Jr. *Polar Bear, Polar Bear, What Do You Hear?* Henry Holt and Company, Inc., 1991.
————, and John Archambault. *Here Are My Hands.* Henry Holt and Company, Inc., 1987.
————. *Chicka Chicka Boom Boom.* Simon & Schuster, 1989.

Pomerantz, Charlotte. *The Piggy in the Puddle.* Macmillan, 1974.

Dr. Seuss. *Green Eggs and Ham.* Random House, 1960.
————. *My Many Colored Days.* Knopf, 1996.

Tafuri, Nancy. *Have You Seen My Duckling?* Greenwillow Books, 1984.

Van Laan, Nancy. *Possum Come a-Knockin'.* Knopf, 1989.

Watanabe, Shigeo. *How Do I Put It On?* Collins, 1979.

Weiss, Nicki. *Sun Sand Sea Sail.* Greenwillow Books, 1989.

Williams, Linda. *The Little Old Lady Who Was Not Afraid of Anything.* Crowell, 1986.

Williams, Vera B. *"More More More" Said the Baby.* Greenwillow Books, 1990.

Winthrop, Elizabeth. *Shoes.* HarperCollins, 1993.

References

CHAPTER 1

McCloskey, Robert. *Blueberries for Sal.* Viking Press, 1948.

Doyle, Charlotte. *Freddie's Spaghetti.* Random House, 1991.

Dr. Seuss. *Green Eggs and Ham.* Random House, 1960.

Martin, Bill, Jr. *Polar Bear, Polar Bear, What Do You Hear?* Henry Holt and Company, Inc., 1991.

CHAPTER 2

Sendak, Maurice. *Where the Wild Things Are.* HarperCollins, 1963.

Cohen, Miriam. *When Will I Read?* Dell, 1977.

Ga'g, Wanda. *Millions of Cats.* Coward McCann, 1928.

Brown, Margaret Wise. *The Runaway Bunny.* Harper, 1942.

White, E. B. *Charlotte's Web.* Harper, 1952.

CHAPTER 3

Brown, Margaret Wise. *Goodnight Moon.* Harper, 1947.

Bissex, Glenda. *Gnys at Wrk.* Harvard University Press, 1980.

Rosenthal, Nadine. *Speaking of Reading.* Heinemann, 1995.

CHAPTER 4

Martin, Bill, Jr., and John Archambault. *Here Are My Hands.* Henry Holt and Company, Inc., 1987.

Clark, Margaret M. Young. *Fluent Readers: What Can They Teach Us?* Heinemann, 1976.

Taylor, Denny, and Catherine Dorsey-Gaines. *Growing Up Literate.* Heinemann, 1988.

CHAPTER 5

Clay, Marie M. *I Can Read!* (video). Heinemann (Distributor), 1990.

————. *Reading Recovery: A Guidebook for Teachers in Training.* Heinemann, 1993.

Lewis, C. S. *The Lion, the Witch, and the Wardrobe.* Macmillan, 1950.

Rigg, Pat and Allen, Virginia G., eds. *When They Don't All Speak English: Integrating the ESL Student into the Regular Classroom.* National Council of Teachers of English, 1989.

CHAPTER 6

Ashton-Warner, Sylvia. *Teacher.* Simon & Schuster, 1963.

Matson, Barbara. "The Harvard Education Letter." March/April 1996.

Honig, Bill. *Teaching Our Children to Read: The Role of Skills in a Comprehensive Reading Program.* Corwin Pr., 1996.

AFTERWORD

Katz, Lilian G. "Early Education: What Should Young Children Be Doing" (Chapter 9) in Kagan, Sharon L., and Zigler, Edward F., eds., *Early Schooling: The National Debate.* Yale University Press, 1987.

Gardner, Howard. *Frames of Mind: The Theory of Multiple Intelligences.* Basic Books, Inc., 1983.

Edwards, Carolyn, et al., eds. *The Hundred Languages of Children: The Reggio Emilia Approach to Early Childhood Education.* Ablex, 1993.

Katz, Lilian G. and Chard, Sylvia C. *Engaging Children's Minds: The Project Approach.* Ablex, 1989.